MERCHANT PALACES

Liverpool and Wirral Mansions Photographed by Bedford Lemere & Co.

Joseph Sharples

The Bluecoat Press

Published by The Bluecoat Press, Liverpool
Designed by LawnCreative, Liverpool
Printed by Grafo, Spain

ISBN 9781904438 50 2

Photographers of Liverpool Series

The Bluecoat Press is publishing a landmark series of titles concerned with the way photographers have interpreted the people and cityscape of Liverpool. There are an impressive number of photographs in collections, private and public, which contribute substantially to our understanding of the growth and shape of the city and each volume in this series will reproduce images from these important archives.

Front cover: The music room, Thornton Manor, 1903
Back cover: A hall doorway, 31 Croxteth Road, September 1891
Right: Mrs Blackler's bathroom, Park Lea, 1916

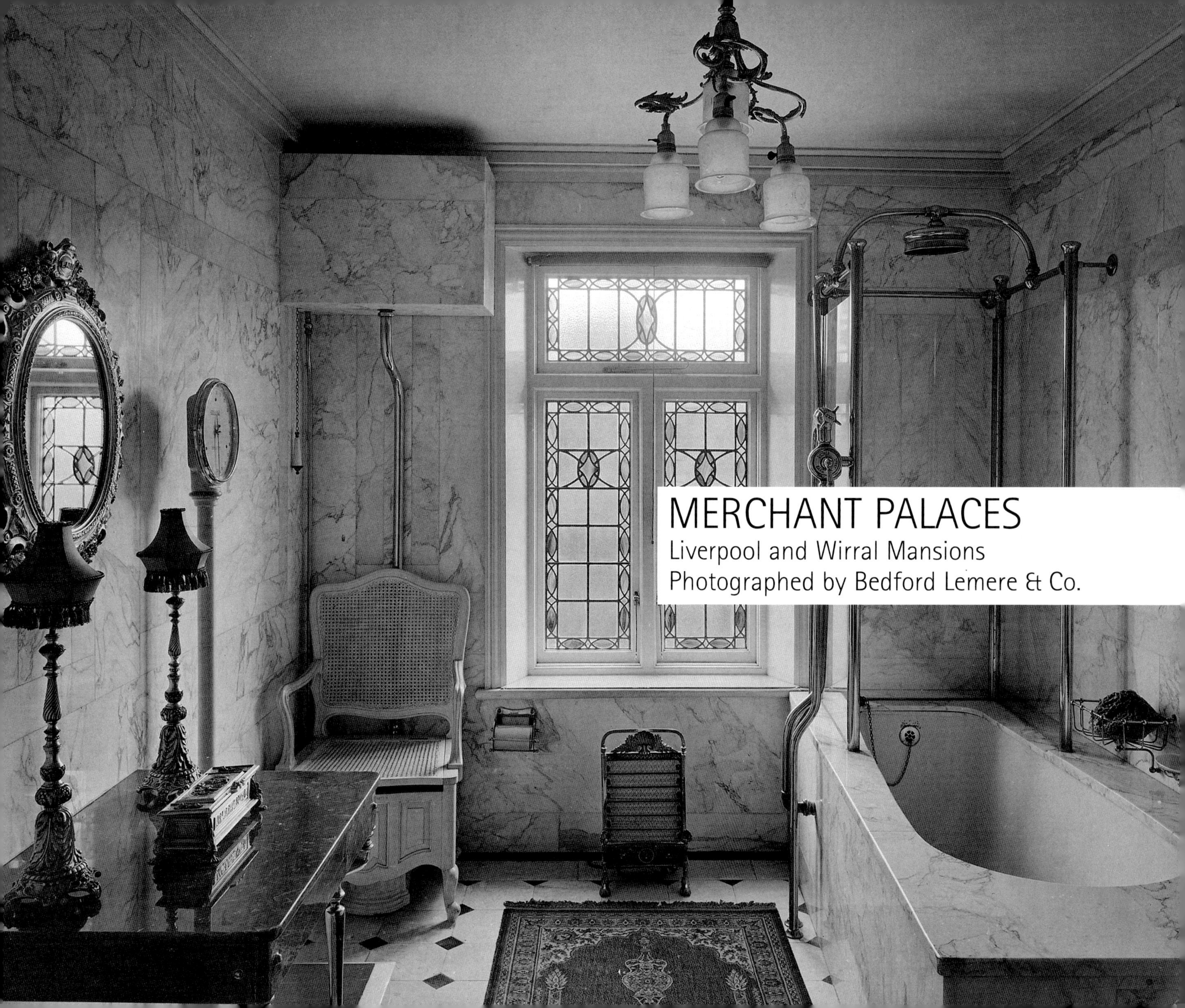

MERCHANT PALACES

Liverpool and Wirral Mansions Photographed by Bedford Lemere & Co.

Introduction

The photographs

The photographs in this book were taken between 1888 and 1916 by the London-based firm Bedford Lemere & Co. Most are the work of Harry Bedford Lemere (1864-1944), one of the best architectural photographers of his day. He travelled the country taking pictures of opulent houses, sometimes as a record for their owners, sometimes for professional decorators or architects. The wealth of late Victorian and Edwardian Liverpool often brought him to Merseyside. He used natural light rather than flash, and long exposure times meant he rarely included figures. Nevertheless, his sharply focused pictures are full of telling personal details, and they give a vivid insight into the private world of Liverpool's elite. His daily work books survive, so in most cases we know exactly when, where and for whom the pictures were taken.

The houses

'Crowds of comfortable and luxurious villas', wrote the journalist Patricius Walker in 1873, 'besprinkle the country for miles round Liverpool, inhabited by ship-owners, ship-insurers, corn merchants, cotton brokers, emigrant agents, &c., &c., men with "one foot on sea, and one on shore," yet to one thing constant ever – namely, money-making – and therein duly successful.' Liverpool, the second port of the British Empire, was at the height of its prosperity when these photographs were taken, and most of its leading citizens were successful merchants, dealing in goods imported through the docks. Others who derived their wealth from the maritime economy included lawyers, stockbrokers, bankers and manufacturers in food processing and the chemical industry.

During the nineteenth century these rich businessmen increasingly chose to live at a distance from the noisy, dirty, crowded centre of Liverpool, where their offices were situated and where they made their money. They became commuters, moving to suburbs where they could live in bigger houses and enjoy open space, clean air and peace. Favoured locations included private estates like Fulwood Park and Sandfield Park, containing clusters of substantial villas such as Park Lea (plates 46-48). From the 1870s the newly laid out Sefton Park provided a green oasis in south Liverpool, which became the focus of a high-class residential area within easy reach of the city centre. The wealthiest could afford even larger mansions on the fringes of the city, such as Broughton Hall (plates 3 & 4), set in their own extensive grounds. Though private carriages were important for commuting, public transport was also used by the merchant class, and it encouraged the spread of suburban living. The railway enabled the development of the affluent seaside suburb of Blundellsands from the 1860s onwards, where the timber merchant Joseph Gardner lived at Uplands (plate 45). Later, improved rail links made the Wirral more accessible, bringing houses like T.H. Ismay's Dawpool (plates 23-25) and William E. Cain's Wilton Grange (plates 43 & 44) within easy reach of the city.

Merchants' houses reflected both the social and business lives of their occupiers – the two were often closely intertwined. Dinner parties were an important way for merchants to entertain their business associates, and dining rooms and drawing rooms, such as Richard R. Lockett's at Enmore (plates 27 & 28), were richly decorated. Similarly, entrance halls like those at 4 Croxteth Drive (plate 29), Kiln Hey (plate 5) and Orleans House (plate 50) were designed to receive large numbers of guests and impress them with a sense of the host's social status and commercial success. Music rooms, like William Imrie's at Holmestead (plate 32) and Richard le Doux's at Marlfield (plate 36), were another conspicuous sign of wealth, and could accommodate large gatherings. Billiard rooms (plates 15 & 34), smoking rooms (plates 20 & 22) and libraries (plates 8, 33 & 35) tended to be male preserves, where business could be discussed privately and informally. The generous grounds of bigger mansions provided outdoor space for leisure and recreation. An elaborate conservatory of cast iron and glass – such as S.J. Waring's at Palmyra (plate 26) or Walter C. Clark's at Orleans House (plate 49) – was often a decorative and costly feature, while extensive glasshouses served a practical purpose by supplying produce for the table.

In Victorian Liverpool a successful merchant could make a large fortune quickly, and newly acquired wealth was often displayed through the decoration of a showy villa in a fashionable modern suburb. In a poem entitled *Nouveaux Riches*, the Liverpool satirical magazine *Porcupine* (14 December 1867) described the residence of a typical 'knight of cotton':

'His house, in which he's like a stranded fish,
Has all within – without – that heart could wish,
That is, a heart that takes a dear delight
In nice upholsterer's knick-knacks, new and bright,
And heaps of fripperies, not one year old,
And varnished shams and glitter, paint and gold.'

To judge from Bedford Lemere's photographs, the same taste for lavish display was still flourishing thirty or forty years later. Some new houses, such as Richard R. Lockett's Enmore and E.H. Cookson's Kiln Hey, were furnished in Elizabethan, Jacobean and eighteenth-century styles. Among merchants who had 'risen from nothing', this taste for historical styles may show a desire to imitate the trappings of old money, and so appear more respectable in the eyes of established society.

Others had more sophisticated tastes, and patronised progressive architects and designers. A few, such as Dashper Edward Glynn at Sefton House (plate 31), showed an interest in the Arts and Crafts movement with its emphasis on hand craftsmanship. Some, such as John Gray Hill at Mere Hall (plates 41 & 42), were influenced by the ideals of the Aesthetic movement, using antique furniture and oriental carpets and porcelain to create interiors of elegance and refinement. Many Liverpool businessmen, such as William Imrie at Holmestead (plates 32-34), formed ambitious art collections, and some, like the soap manufacturer W.H. Lever at Thornton Manor (plates 37 & 38) and the shipowner T.H. Ismay at Dawpool (plate 24), built special rooms in which to display their pictures. Works from these private collections were sometimes presented or bequeathed to Liverpool's Walker Art Gallery, while Lever chose the best of his collection for the Lady Lever Art Gallery, which he built for his workers at Port Sunlight village.

Decorators and architects

Among the Liverpool decorators who commissioned photographs from Bedford Lemere, the best known is S.J. Waring. As well as keeping a shop in fashionable Bold Street he had workshops in St Anne Street where five hundred staff were said to be employed. In 1893 he opened premises in London, merging with the cabinetmaker Gillow to form Waring & Gillow. The firm had an international reputation, designing interiors for ocean liners, royal yachts and hotels, as well as private houses. Some of the most extraordinary decorative schemes ever recorded by Bedford Lemere were those carried out by another Bold Street firm, Turner, Son & Walker. Established in the early nineteenth century, the business employed over fifty people in its workshops and made a speciality of extravagant draperies. Distinct from the work of decorators like these are interiors designed or coordinated by architects. At Mere Hall, the architect Edmund Kirby worked closely with his client John Gray Hill, ensuring that every detail harmonised to produce an aesthetically satisfying whole, while Richard Norman Shaw and his associate J. Aldam Heaton produced similar results at Dawpool for the Ismays.

Decline

Whatever the taste of their designers or occupiers, all the houses recorded in these photographs illustrate the remarkable concentration of wealth in the hands of Liverpool's commercial elite in the late nineteenth and early twentieth centuries. In this respect, Bedford Lemere's pictures make a telling contrast with those taken by the City Engineer around the same time, which show conditions in Liverpool's notorious slums. When J.A. Picton described the affluent houses around Prince's Park in 1871 – 'ormolu tables, walls lined with pictures, well furnished sideboards, and damask curtains' – he drew the same inevitable comparison: 'Alas! That there should be such a reverse to the picture; that there may be found in the same town districts where fever is ever hovering, marking out its daily victims, where the murky alley and squalid court poison with their fetid atmosphere the wretched occupants who huddle together for shelter. [...] The contrasts of modern society are a fruitful theme for speculation, and demand the earnest attention of the statesman and philanthropist.'

These contrasts started to become less extreme after the First World War. Large houses were increasingly difficult to keep up as the supply of domestic servants dwindled, and at the same time Liverpool's declining economic importance meant that wealthy families left the area. The sites of more and more suburban mansions were sold off for building land. Some were replaced by groups of comparatively modest middle class homes. Others, such as Norris Green (plates 21 & 22), were acquired by Liverpool Corporation and their grounds turned into public parks or built over with public housing. Others again were converted to institutional uses. But it was after the Second World War, when the architecture of the city's Victorian heyday had become deeply unfashionable, that some of its most distinguished houses were destroyed. By the late 1950s it was planned to demolish all the nineteenth-century villas bordering Sefton Park and replace them with tower and slab blocks, a proposal that was partly carried out.

In 1904, when Charles Reilly arrived from London to take up his post as professor of architecture at the University of Liverpool, he was struck by the sheer number of mansions in the affluent suburbs. By the time he published his autobiography *Scaffolding in the Sky* in 1938, however, the scene had changed completely. 'The south end of Liverpool had an extraordinary number of large houses and grounds at the beginning of the century', he wrote. 'There were great areas like Mossley Hill and Aigburth where there were hardly any small houses and where one fine estate joined another. Now they have nearly all been cut up for building.' But Reilly's regret for this lost era of elegant living was tempered with a sense of its social injustices: 'The disappearance [...] of the big houses and estates in Liverpool, it must be remembered, is contemporary with the great attack on the slums. Thirty years ago they existed almost side by side as if dependent for their existence one on the other, as no doubt in a sense they were.'

A century now separates us from the Liverpool described by Reilly, and an effort of imagination is needed to appreciate the wealth of the region's late-Victorian and Edwardian merchants. The sumptuous furnishings are long gone – and in many cases the houses too – but Bedford Lemere's extraordinary photographs survive to document this vanished world of privilege.

Further reading

N. Cooper, *The Opulent Eye*, 1976
P. de Figueiredo and J. Treuherz, *Cheshire Country Houses*, 1988
B. G. Orchard, *Liverpool's Legion of Honour*, 1893
J.A. Picton, *Memorials of Liverpool*, 1871
R. Pollard, *Pevsner Architectural Guides: Lancashire – Liverpool and the South-West*, 2006
Joseph Sharples, *Pevsner Architectural Guides: Liverpool*, 2004
Patricius Walker, *Rambles*, 1873

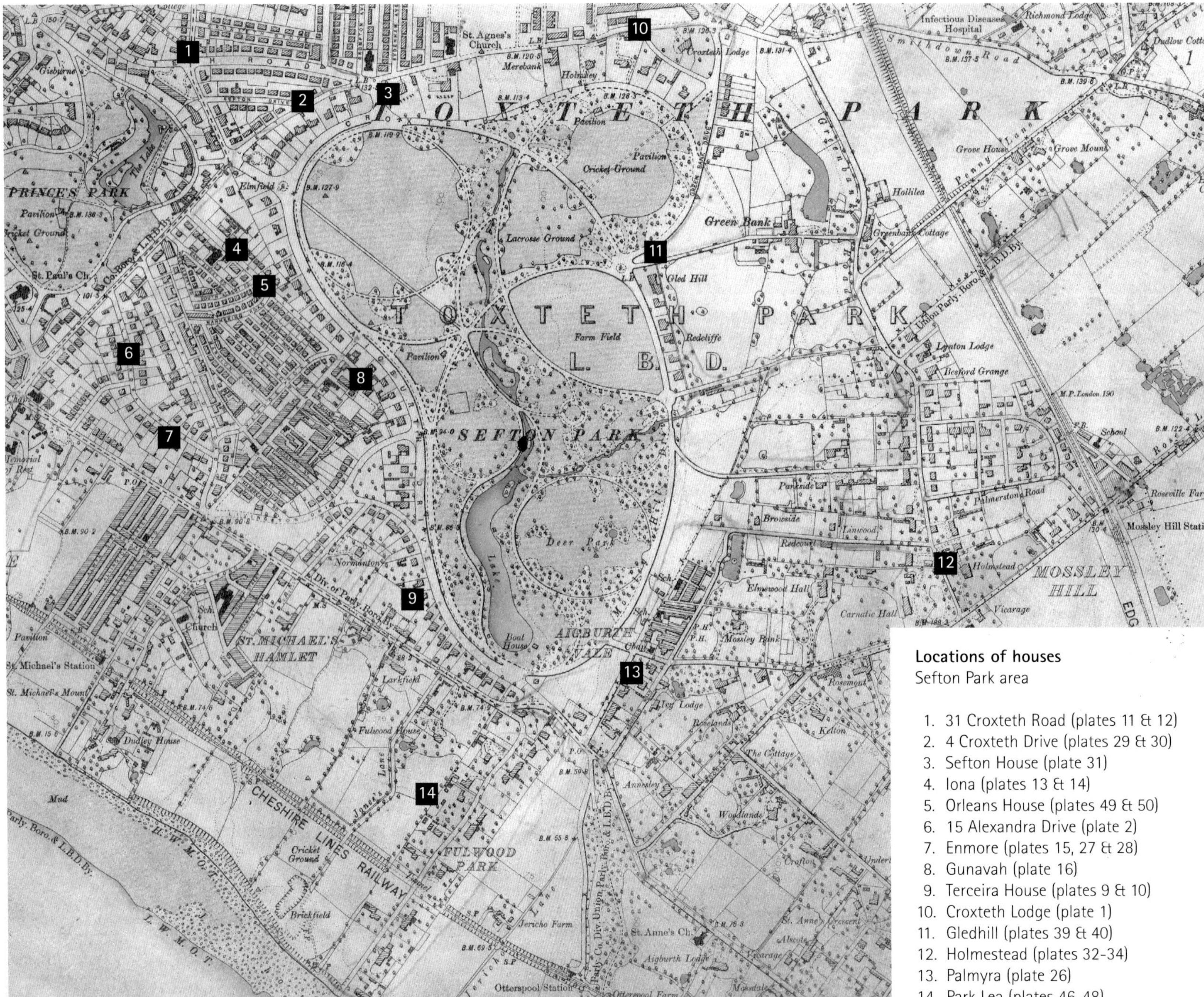

Ordnance Survey, 1894

Locations of houses
Sefton Park area

1. 31 Croxteth Road (plates 11 & 12)
2. 4 Croxteth Drive (plates 29 & 30)
3. Sefton House (plate 31)
4. Iona (plates 13 & 14)
5. Orleans House (plates 49 & 50)
6. 15 Alexandra Drive (plate 2)
7. Enmore (plates 15, 27 & 28)
8. Gunavah (plate 16)
9. Terceira House (plates 9 & 10)
10. Croxteth Lodge (plate 1)
11. Gledhill (plates 39 & 40)
12. Holmestead (plates 32-34)
13. Palmyra (plate 26)
14. Park Lea (plates 46-48)

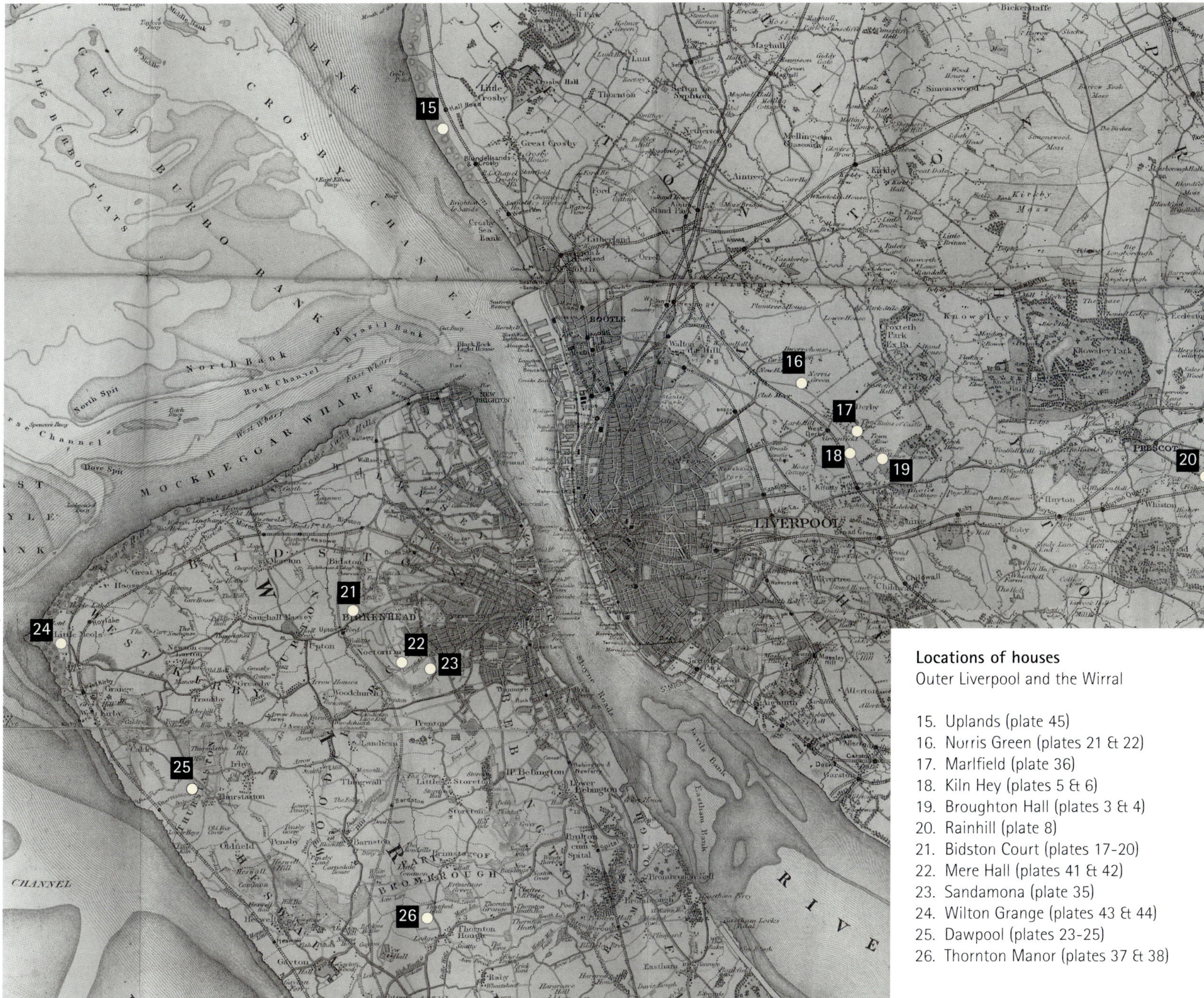

Bacon's Cycling and Touring Map, 1910

Locations of houses
Outer Liverpool and the Wirral

15. Uplands (plate 45)
16. Norris Green (plates 21 & 22)
17. Marlfield (plate 36)
18. Kiln Hey (plates 5 & 6)
19. Broughton Hall (plates 3 & 4)
20. Rainhill (plate 8)
21. Bidston Court (plates 17-20)
22. Mere Hall (plates 41 & 42)
23. Sandamona (plate 35)
24. Wilton Grange (plates 43 & 44)
25. Dawpool (plates 23-25)
26. Thornton Manor (plates 37 & 38)

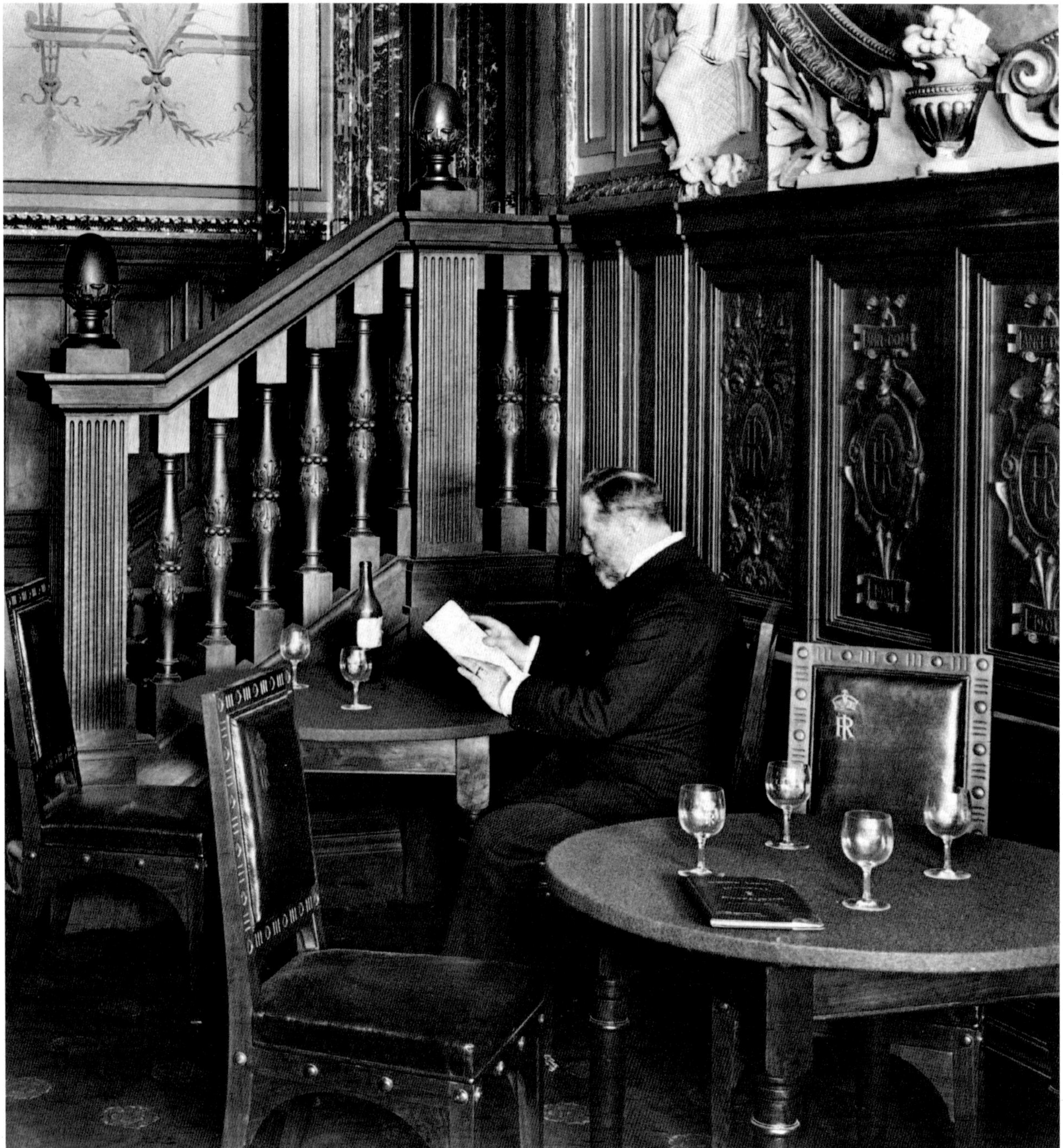

Harry Bedford Lemere, Imperial Restaurant, Regent Street, London, 1901 (BL 16387/9)

List of plates

1. Window recess and screen in the drawing room of Croxteth Lodge, Ullet Road, Sefton Park, 15 November 1887 (BL 8473)

The core of Croxteth Lodge seems to be an early-nineteenth-century house dating from before the creation of Sefton Park, but in its present form the building looks largely Victorian. The photograph records a decorative scheme carried out by S.J. Waring & Sons for the shipowner and merchant William Richard Jones. Screens such as this, incorporating stained glass and curtains, were a fashionable way of creating rich spatial effects and diffusing daylight.

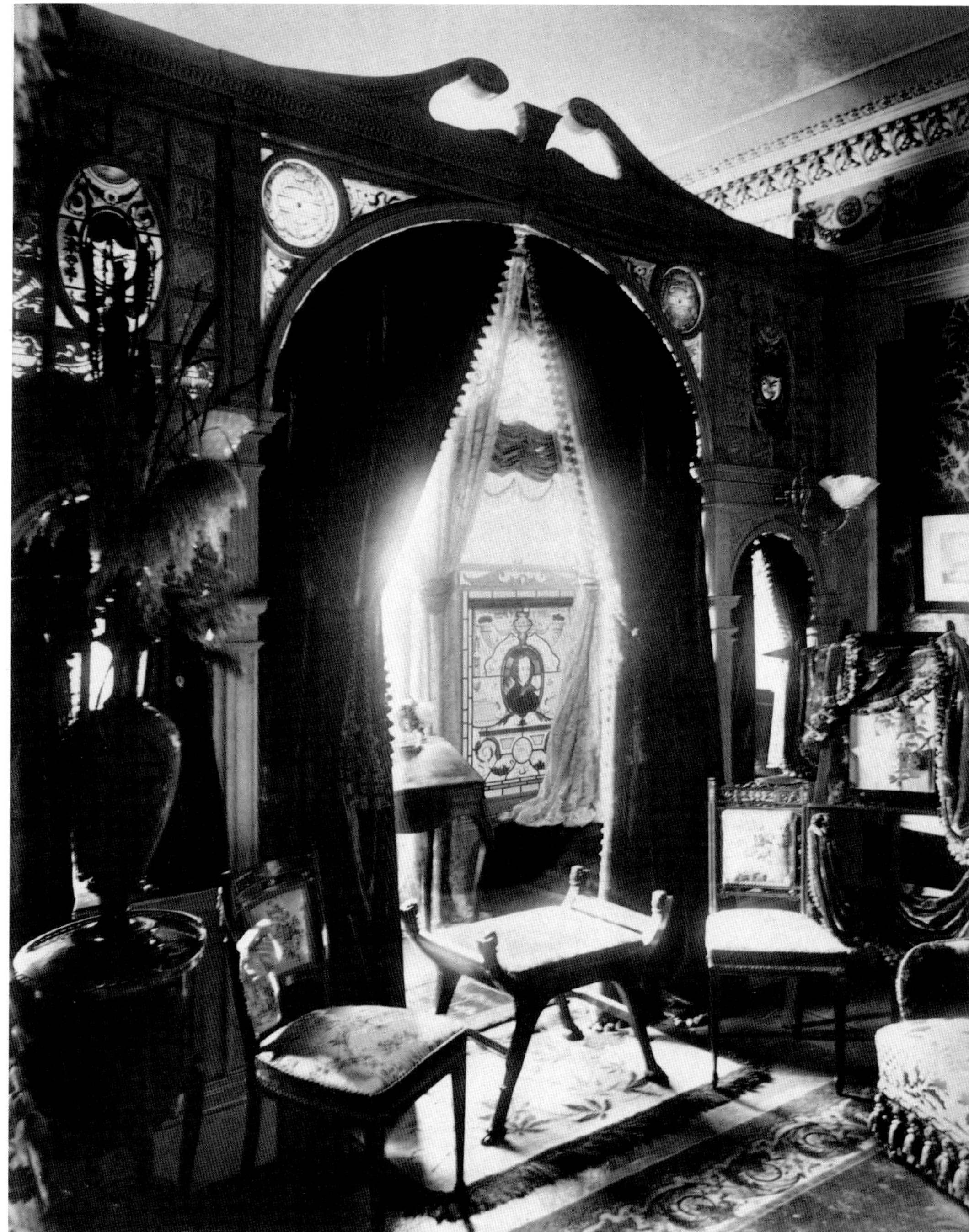

2. A bedroom at 15 Alexandra Drive, Sefton Park, 18 June 1888 (BL 8790)

Alexandra Drive was laid out soon after the 1863 marriage of the Prince of Wales and Princess Alexandra. Predating Sefton Park by a few years, it was an extension to the villa district round neighbouring Prince's Park. When this photograph was taken number 15 was lived in by Alexandre Manbre, a French-born sugar manufacturer and senior partner in the Liverpool Saccharine Company. Whoever occupied this bedroom appears to have been an amateur naturalist: shells and pieces of coral are displayed on the cabinet in the corner, which is open to reveal sliding trays of specimens; a pair of shark's jaws hangs on the wall above; and on the table between the door and the wardrobe there is a large mounted crab.

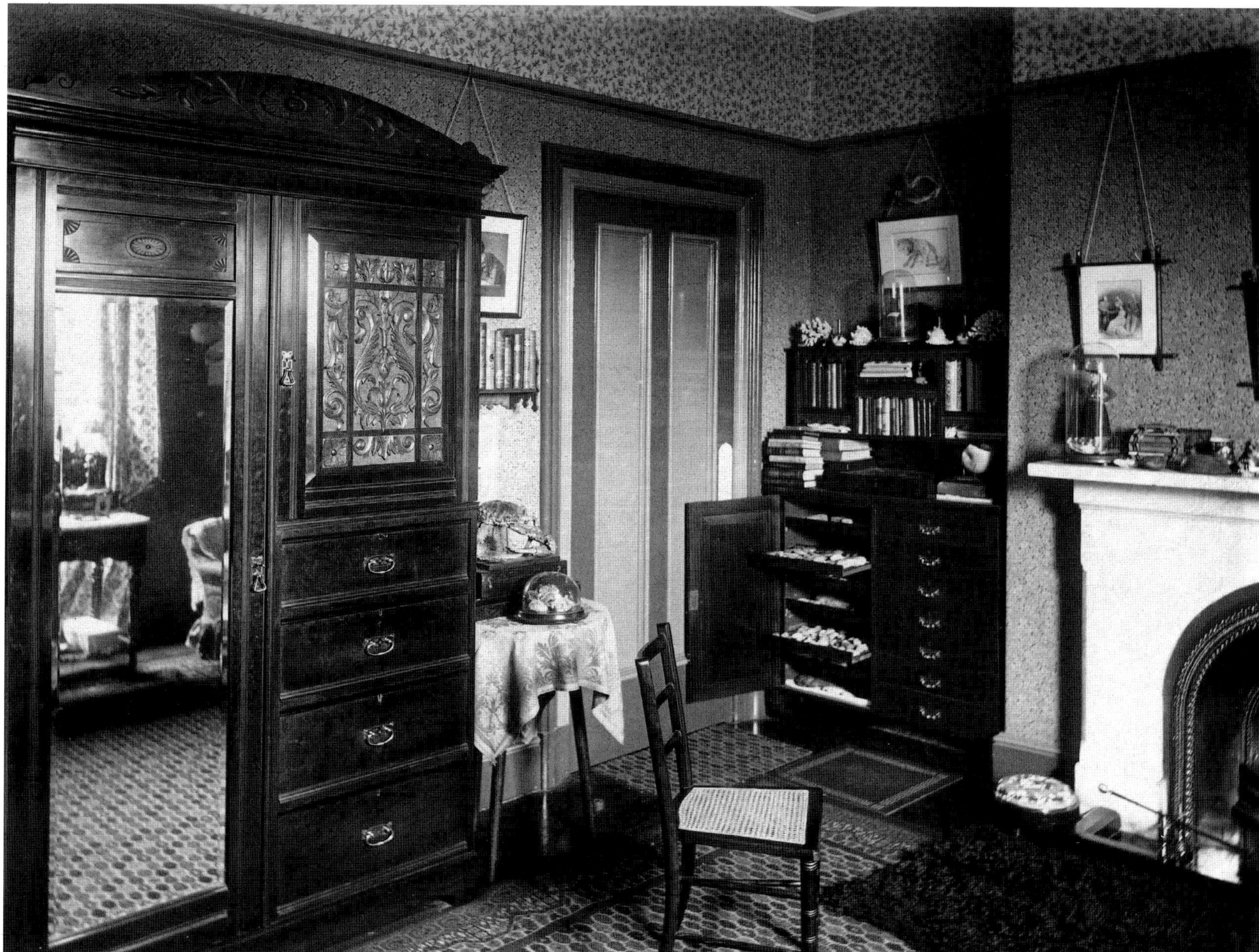

3. The dining room at Broughton Hall, Yew Tree Lane, West Derby, 21 June 1888 (BL 8801)

Built around 1858-9, the large Gothic Revival mansion of Broughton Hall was designed by Walter Scott for the merchant Gustavus C. Schwabe. It was over a game of billiards here that Schwabe suggested to Thomas Henry Ismay the idea of a new transatlantic steamship line, with vessels supplied by Harland and Wolff of Belfast. Schwabe, who was Wolff's uncle, promised to invest in it, and the result was the Oceanic Steam Navigation Company, subsequently known as the White Star Line.

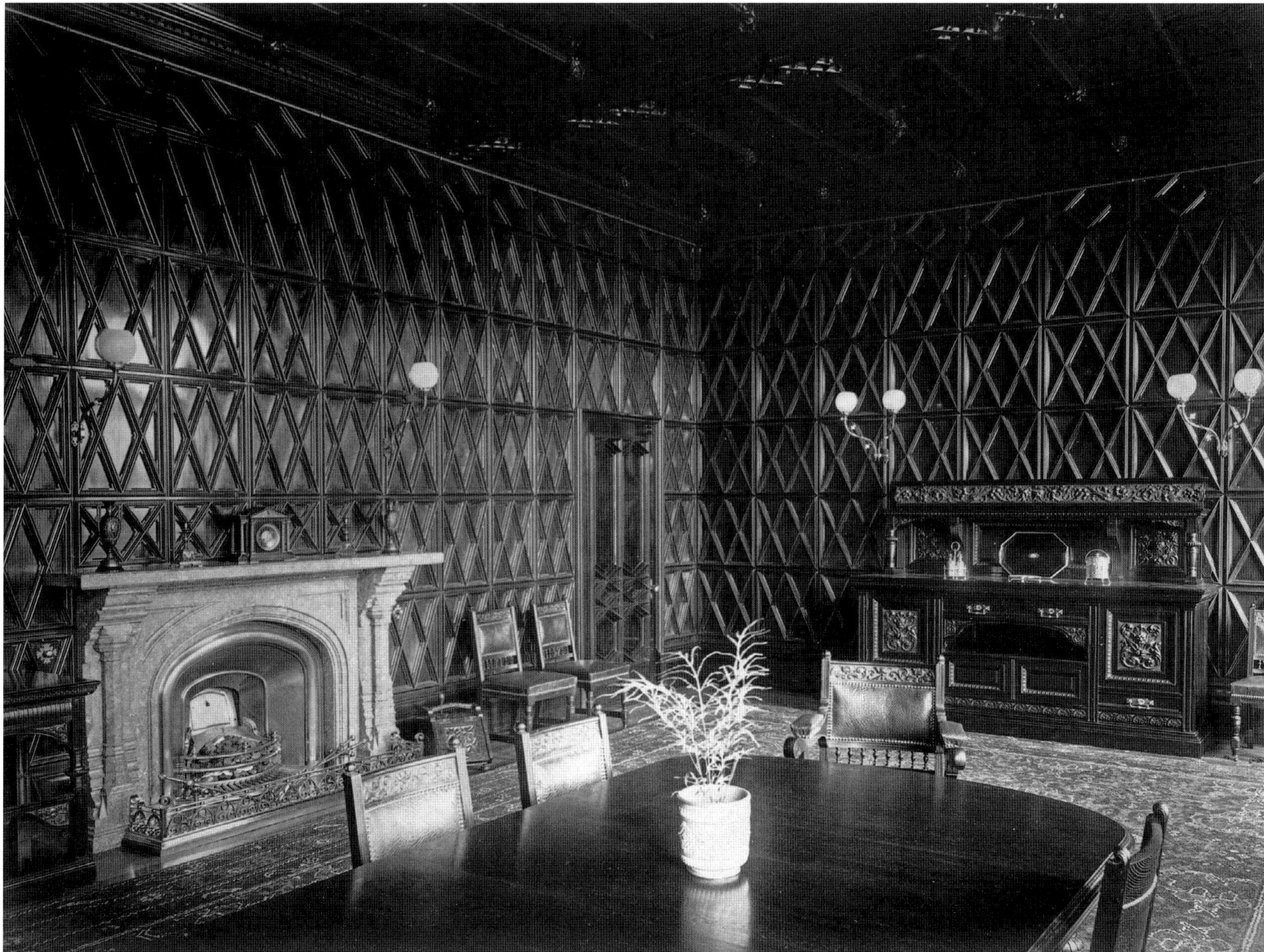

4. Broughton Hall, 21 June 1888 (BL 8806)

By the time this photograph was taken Broughton was occupied by Alfred Morrison Turner, an East India merchant and sugar refiner with offices at 6 Dale Street. He was a director of the Liverpool and London and Globe Insurance Co, and of Parr's Bank. It is presumably Turner's three children – Horace, Edith and Alfred – playing on the lawn with their mother.

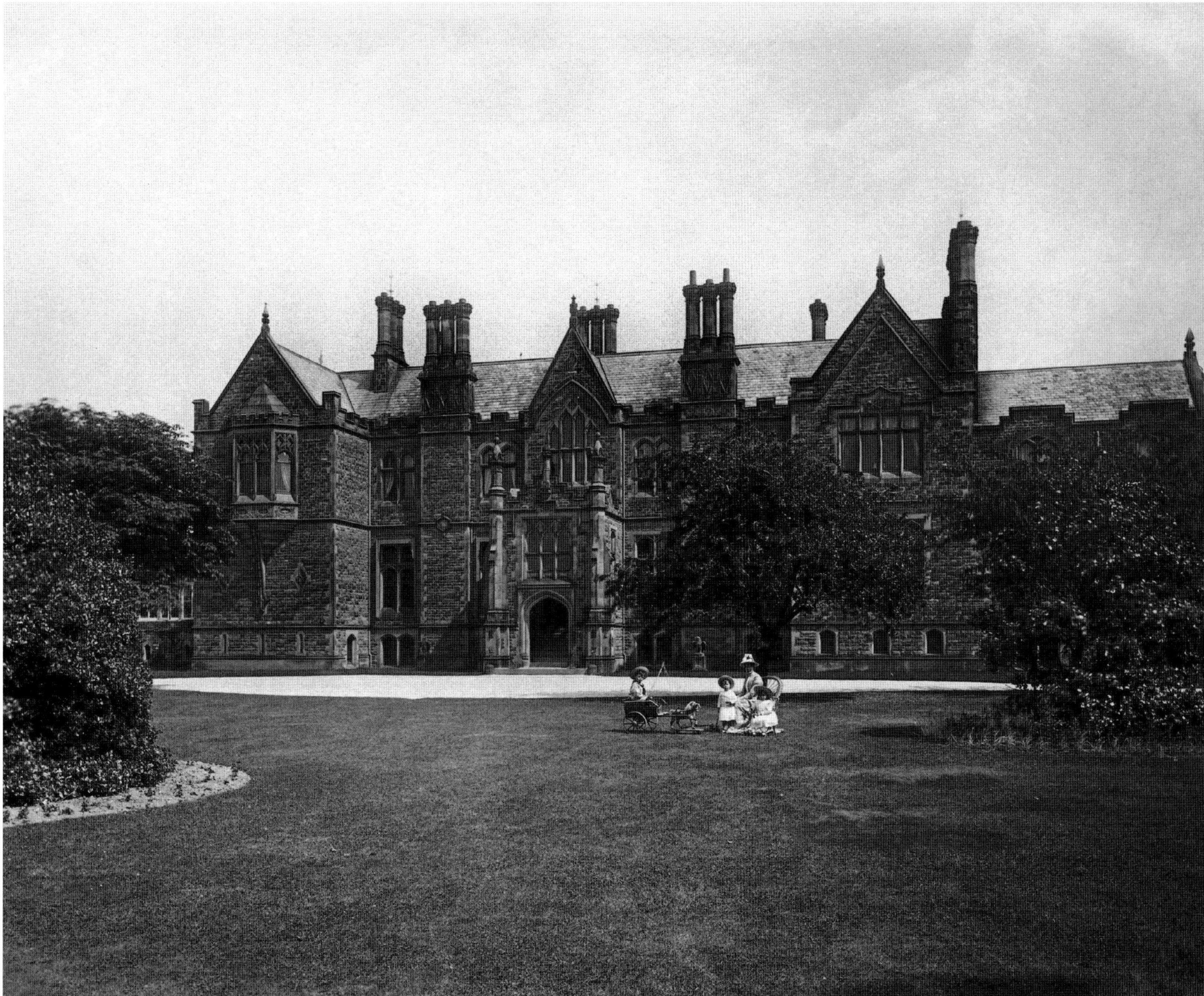

5. The vestibule, Kiln Hey, Sandfield Park, West Derby, 7 September 1888 (BL 8931)

The home of Edward Hatton Cookson, a West Africa merchant who was elected a Conservative councillor in 1884. He acquired Kiln Hey the following year, and promptly doubled it in size, no doubt because his new position in public life required him to entertain on a grander scale. One of the additions he made was this very large and substantially furnished vestibule for receiving guests.

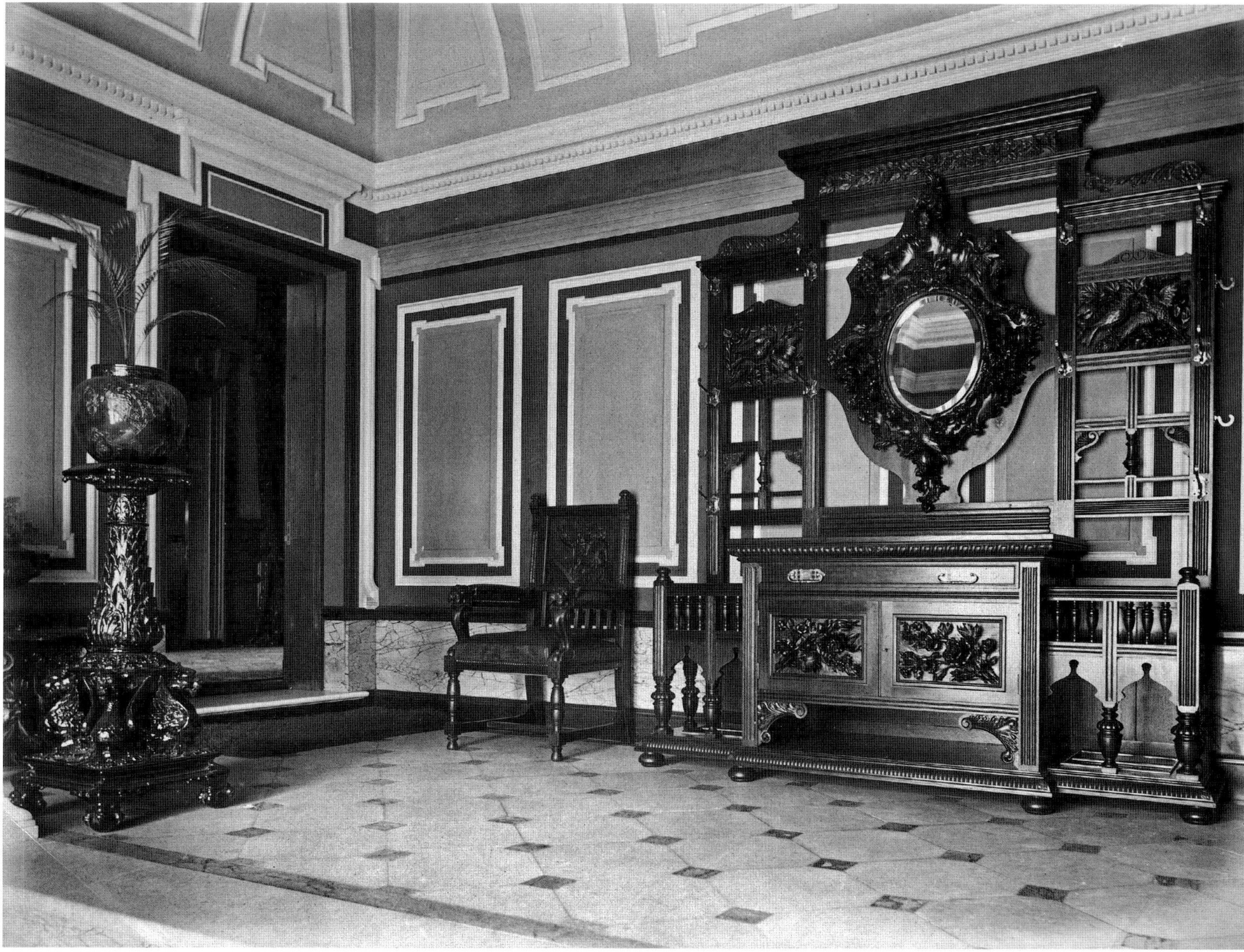

22

6. The drawing room, Kiln Hey, 7 September 1888 (BL 8936)

Edward Hatton Cookson became mayor of Liverpool in 1888. It seems he had Kiln Hey redecorated by Turner, Son & Walker of Bold Street in anticipation of the hospitality his new role would entail: the interiors were photographed just before he was elected. The drawing room was done in eighteenth-century 'Adams' style, with painted panels modelled on Pompeian murals incorporating figures of the Muses.

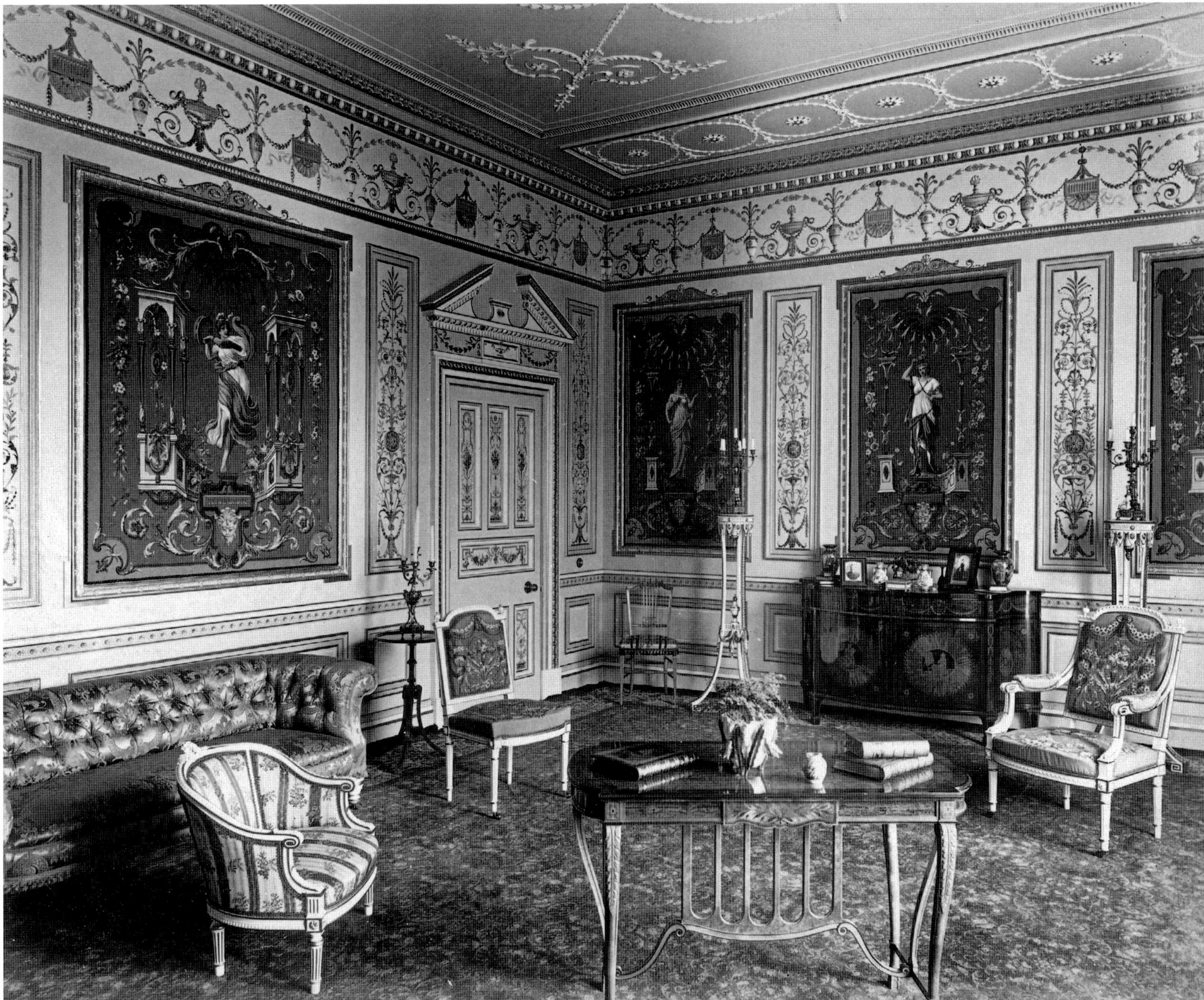

7. Showroom of Messrs Wannop & Son, painters, paper-hangers and decorators, 65 Renshaw Street, 18 June 1890 (BL 10240)

Bedford Lemere sometimes photographed commercial premises. The hanging panels in this decorator's showroom demonstrate some of the Victorian housepainter's skills, including marbling and wood graining. The ceiling, frieze and dado show the late-nineteenth-century taste for Japanese-influenced ornament.

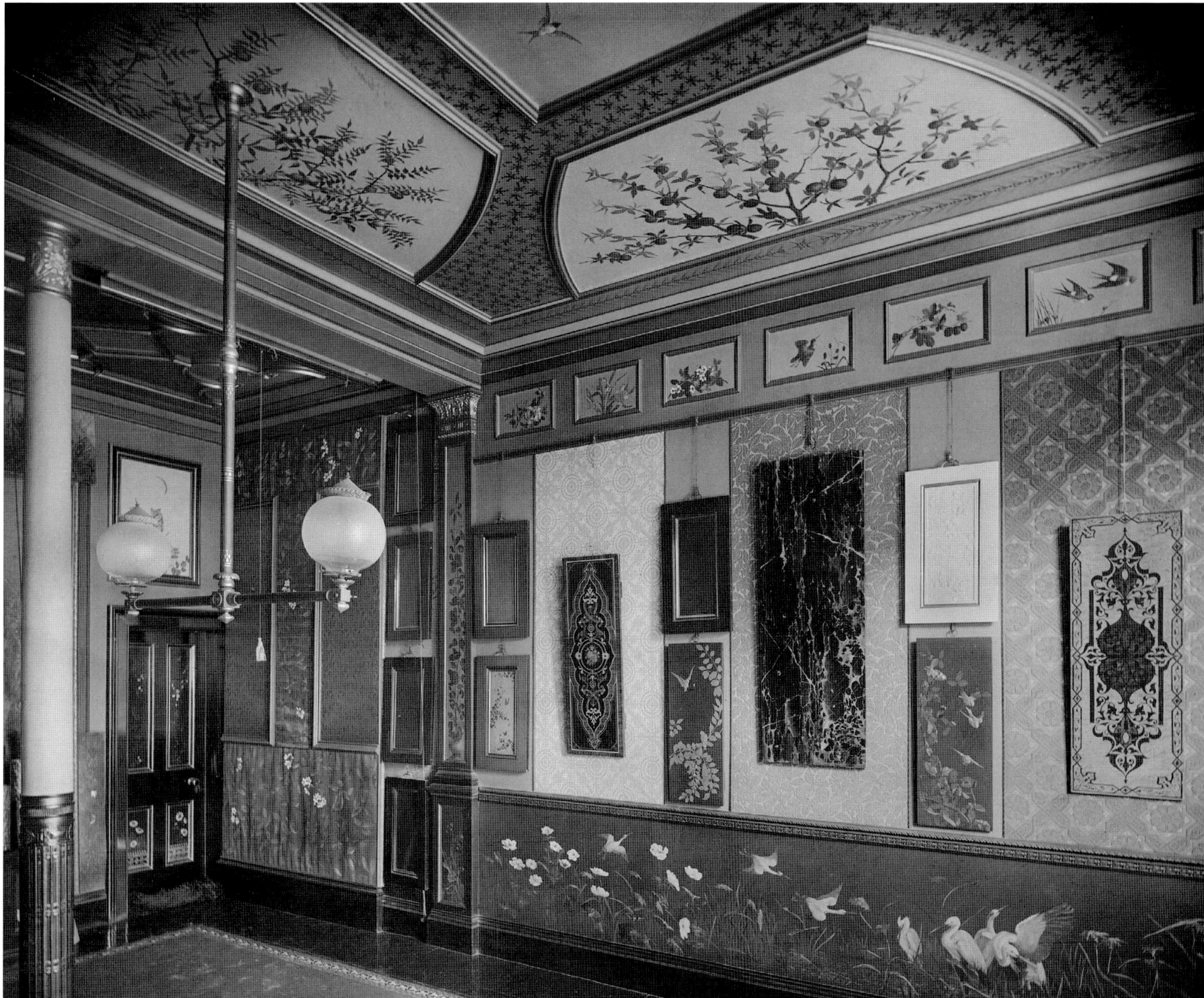

8. Library in an unidentified Merseyside house, possibly at Rainhill, 17 October 1890 (BL 10471)

Unlike many so-called libraries in Liverpool merchants' houses, this is a real scholar's room. Books line the walls, oriental ceramics are displayed as if in a museum, and a microscope under a glass dome stands on the table. The architect was Edmund Rathbone, of the well-known Liverpool family of merchants and philanthropists. In the 1880s he had been associated with the Century Guild, a group of progressive Arts and Crafts designers, and the style of this library is close to the Guild's work. Pattern is confined to the unusual fretwork of the chair backs, and the carpet with its stencilled border. The owner of the house is not known.

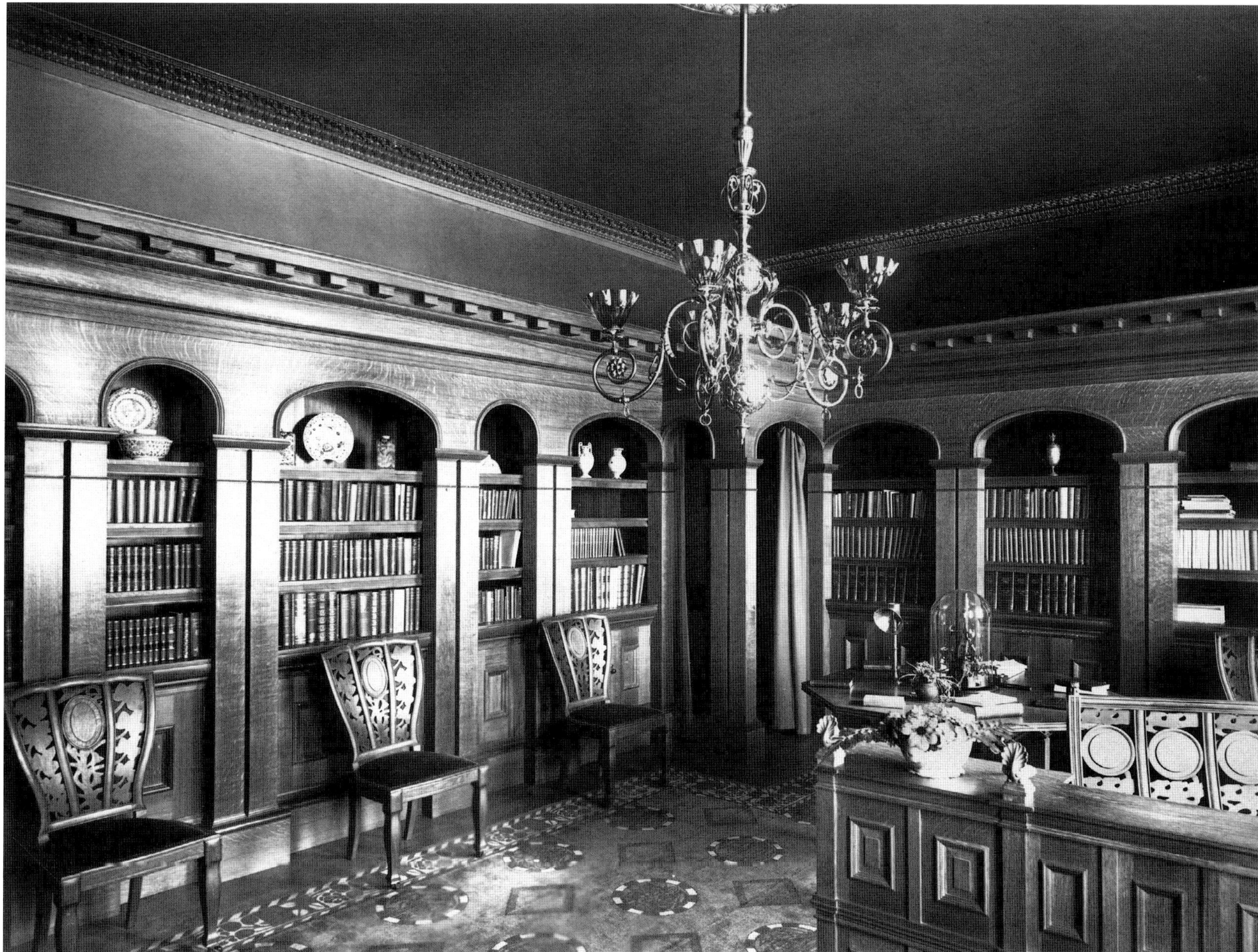

9. The drawing room, Terceira House, Aigburth Drive, September 1891 (BL 11107)

This was the home of Richard Dart, a prosperous fruit broker with Messrs J.C. Houghton & Co in Temple Court. He was elected a Conservative councillor in 1895. The house takes its name from an island in the Azores where fruit was grown for export. It was decorated for Dart by Turner, Son & Walker.

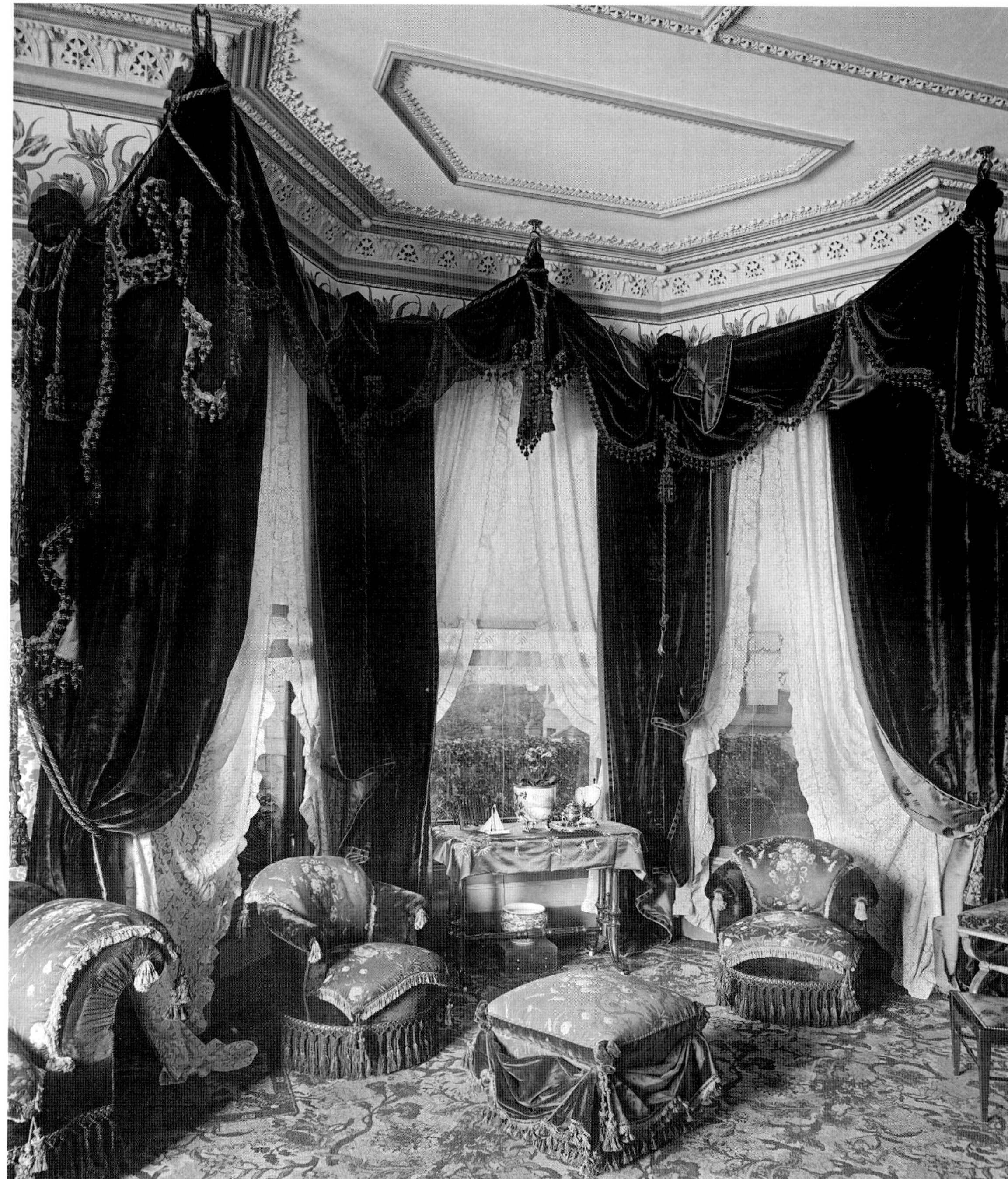

10. The drawing room, Terceira House, September 1891 (BL 11105)

The same room as in plate 9, but looking in the opposite direction. The picture was evidently taken before the onset of Autumn weather, since a display of potted ferns still occupies the fireplace. An engraving of Queen Victoria hangs in pride of place on the far wall, flanked by what are presumably family photographs.

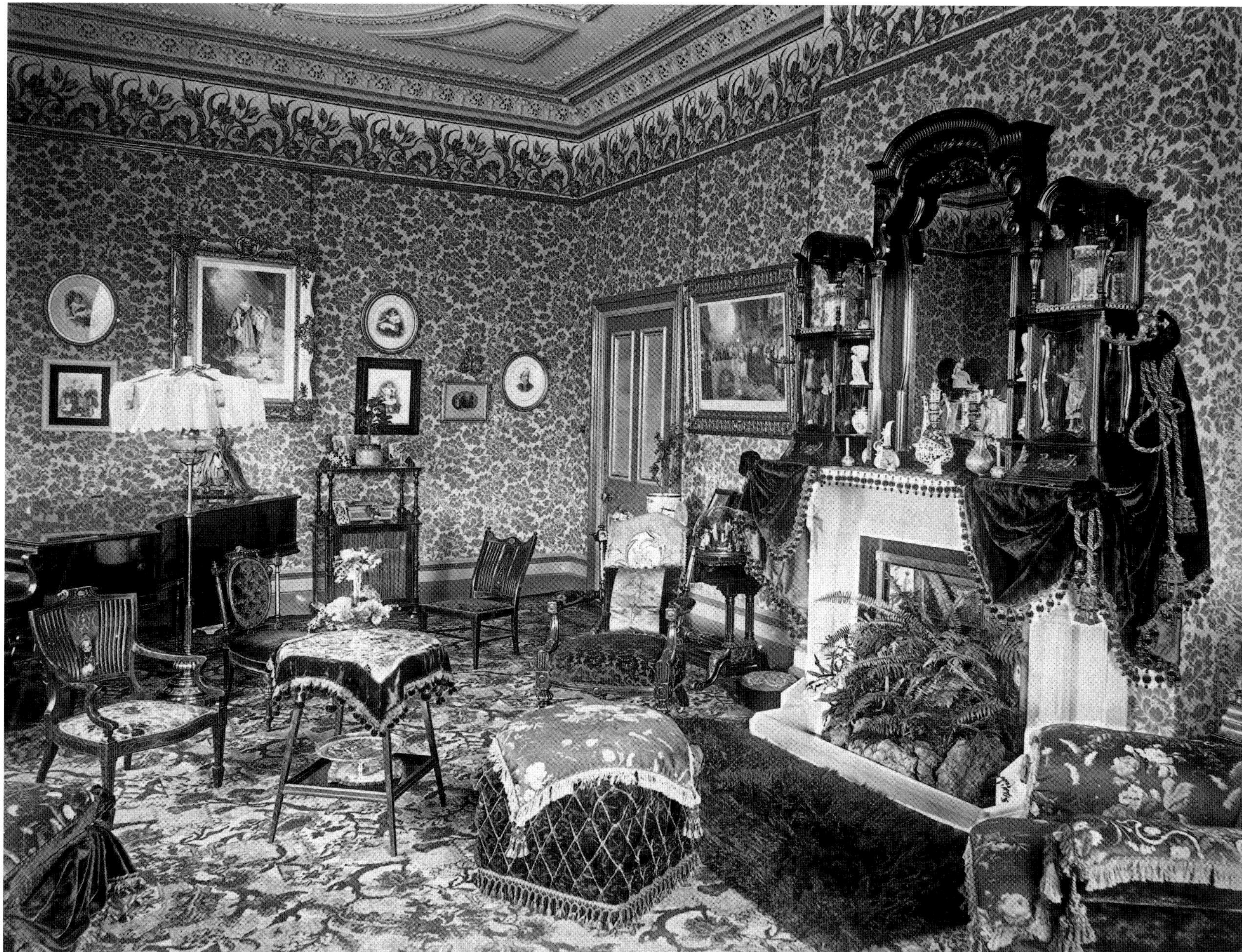

11. A hall doorway, 31 Croxteth Road, September 1891 (BL 11111)

Turner, Son & Walker furnished this house for the merchant Constantine C. Ralli. Sumptuous draperies were a feature throughout, the most spectacular being this portiere or door curtain in the hall. Swags of velvet, heavy with embroidery and fringing, are lashed to an extraordinary framework of halberds and swords. The door would have been used by servants – it led to a pantry – but there is a doorstop to prevent it from being opened too far.

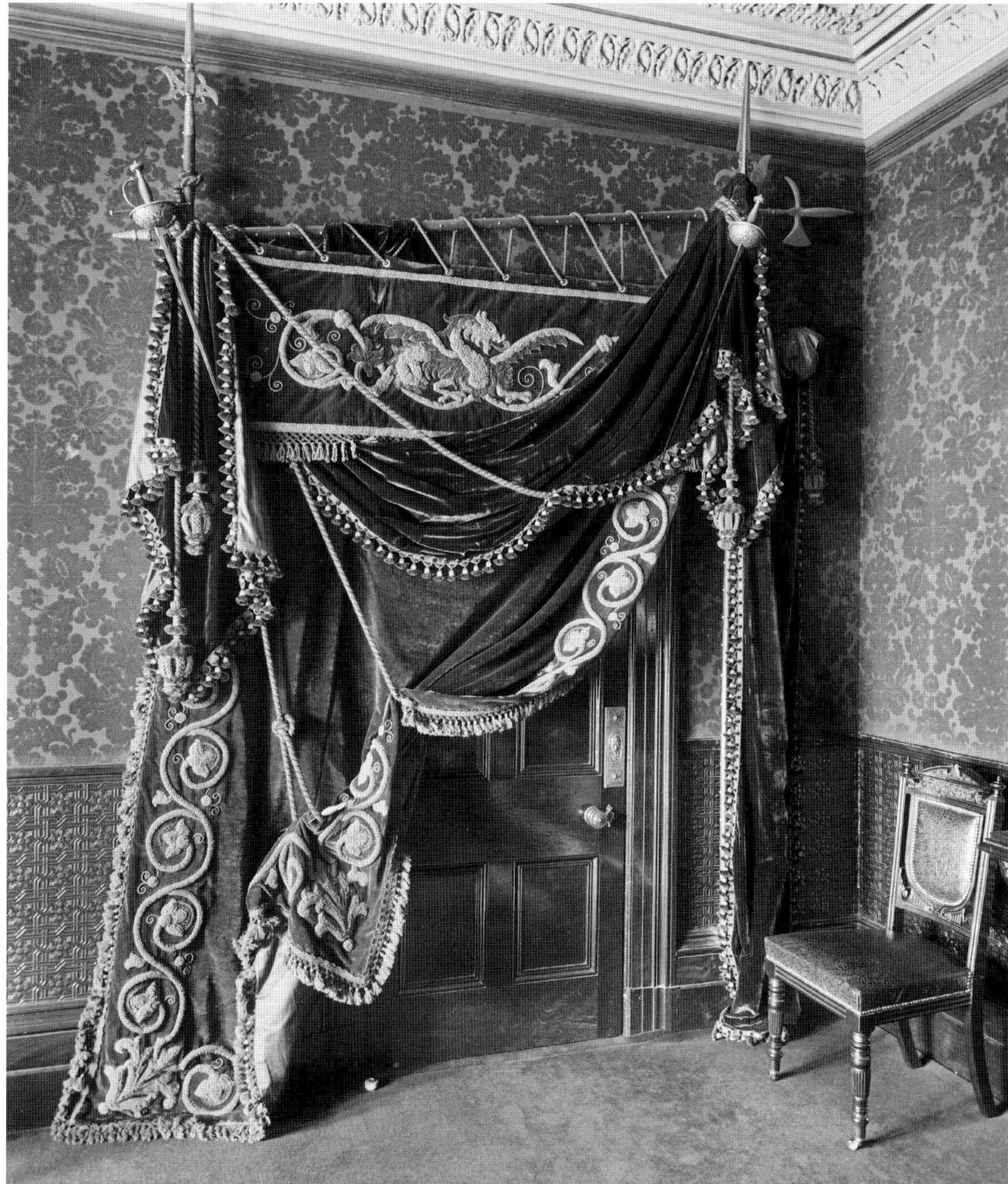

12. The drawing room fireplace, 31 Croxteth Road, September 1891 (BL 11115)

The relatively plain treatment of walls and ceiling means that this remarkable fireplace would have completely dominated the room.

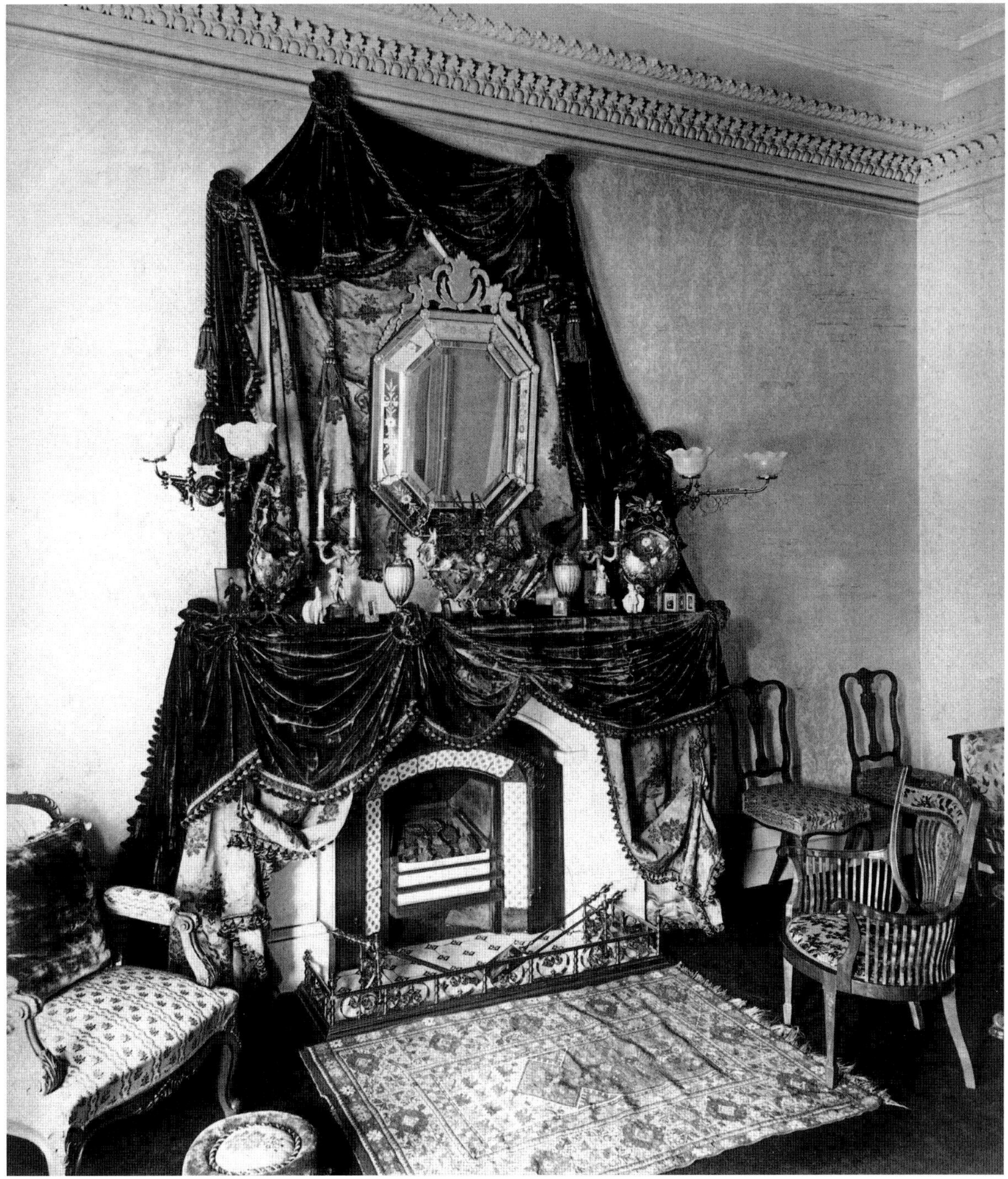

13. The drawing room at Iona, 13 Linnet Lane, Sefton Park, 30 September 1891 (BL 11142)

Iona was furnished by Turner, Son & Walker for the merchant George Constantine Ralli, brother of Constantine C. Ralli of 31 Croxteth Road. Both houses featured lavish draperies. The frieze resembles some of the decorations displayed in Wannop's showroom (see plate 7). The Rallis belonged to Liverpool's Greek community, who were significant players in the port's commercial life. The magnificent Greek Orthodox church at the north end of Princes Road is evidence of their importance. Many of them lived in the leafy drives and avenues around Sefton Park.

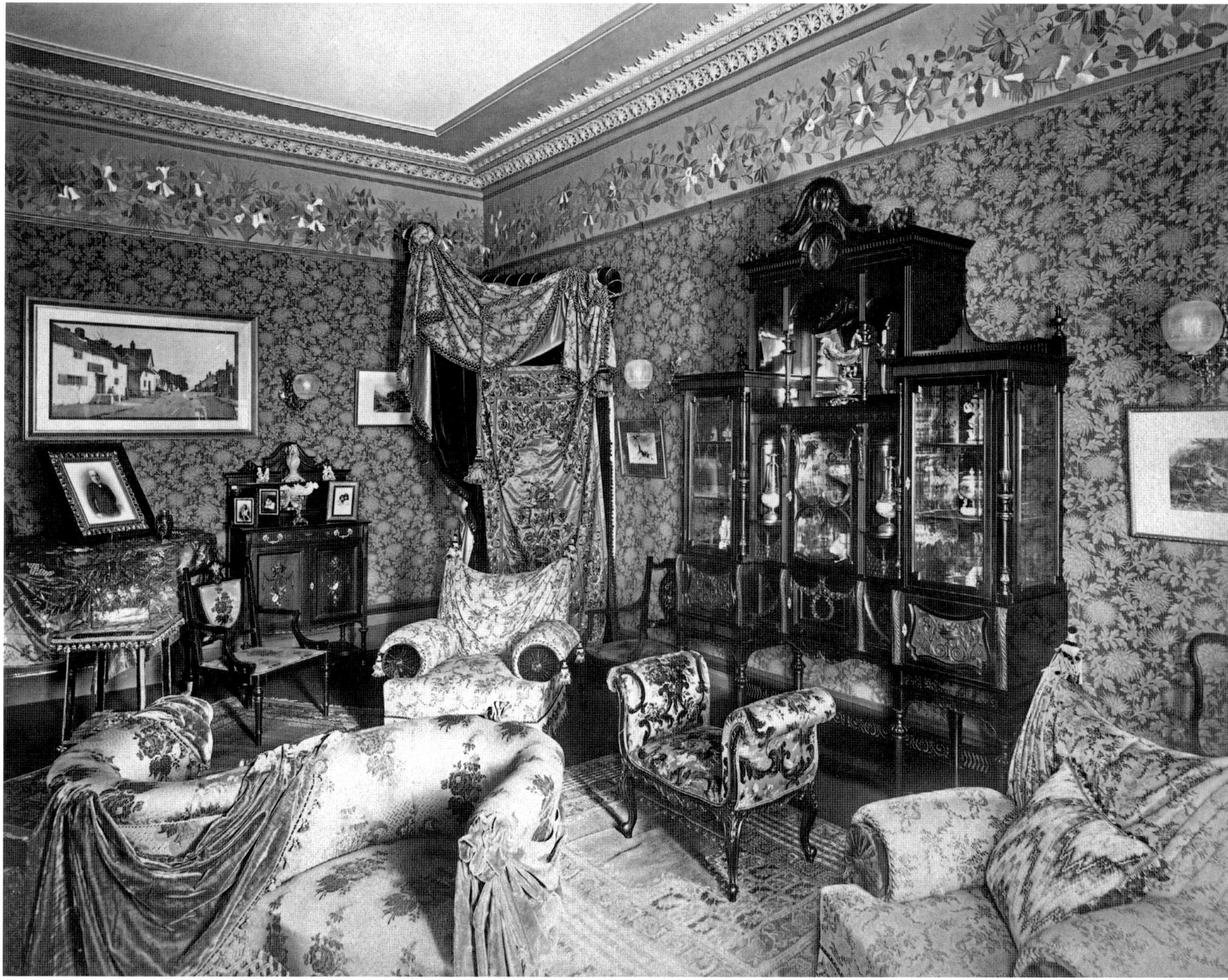

14. A bedroom at Iona, 30 September 1891 (BL 11147)

In their twin Empire-style beds, the Rallis slept in Napoleonic splendour.

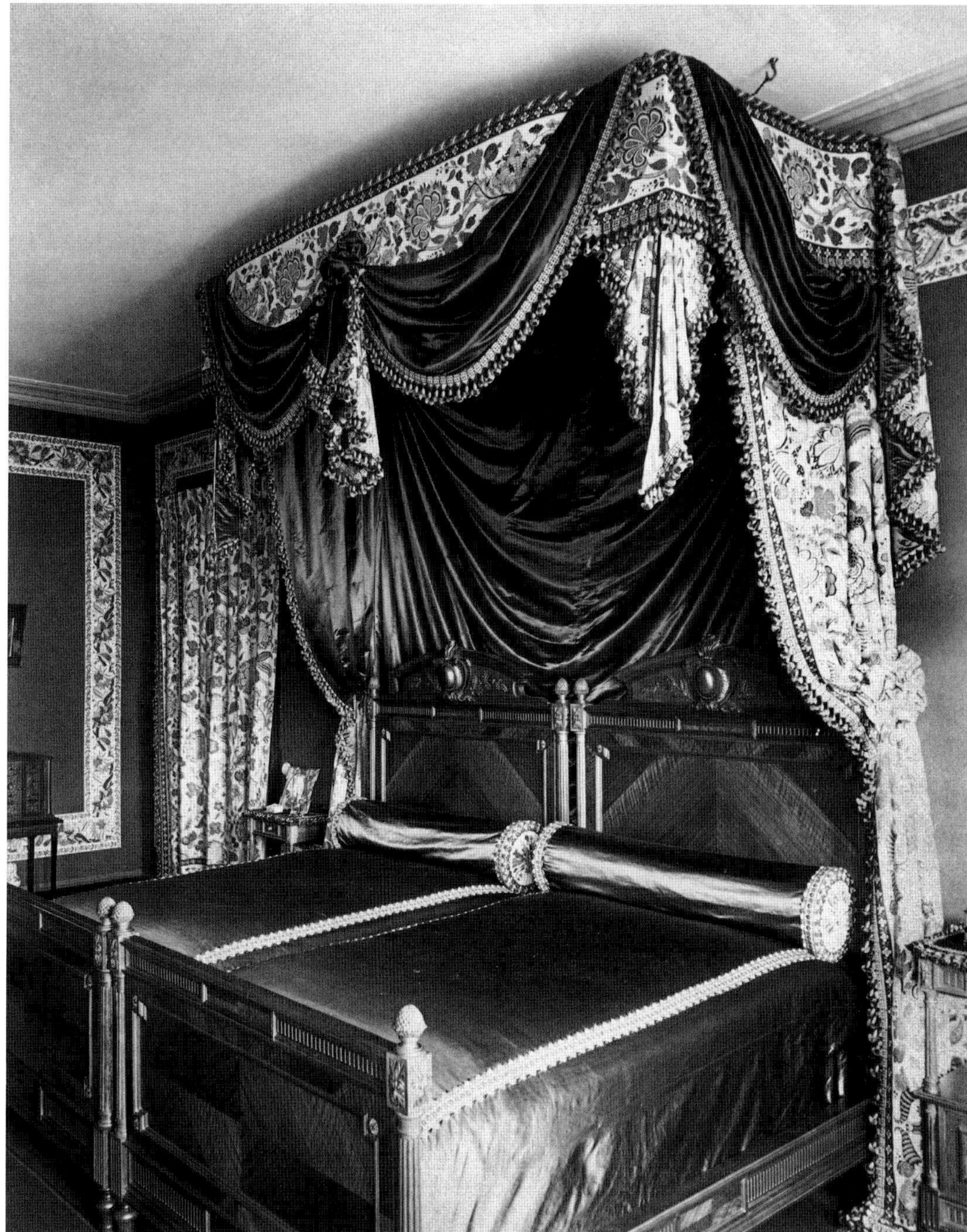

15. The billiard room, Enmore, 34 Alexandra Drive, October 1891 (BL 11226)

Bedford Lemere's photographs of Enmore show a prosperous businessman's house aiming to give an impression of respectable 'old money'. It was the home of Richard R. Lockett, who made a modern fortune in the South American nitrate trade but could trace his family back to the seventeenth century. He moved to Alexandra Drive, just south of Sefton Park, in 1878, and extended the house a number of times. The billiard room is Jacobean in style, and the stag's head gives it a country house feel. As a local magazine observed, 'living in Sefton Park, the *nouveau riche* may be able to encourage the feeling that he is living in his ancestral domain, that his foot is on his native heath, and his name anything you like that is antique and romantic' (*Liverpool Review*, 29 May 1886).

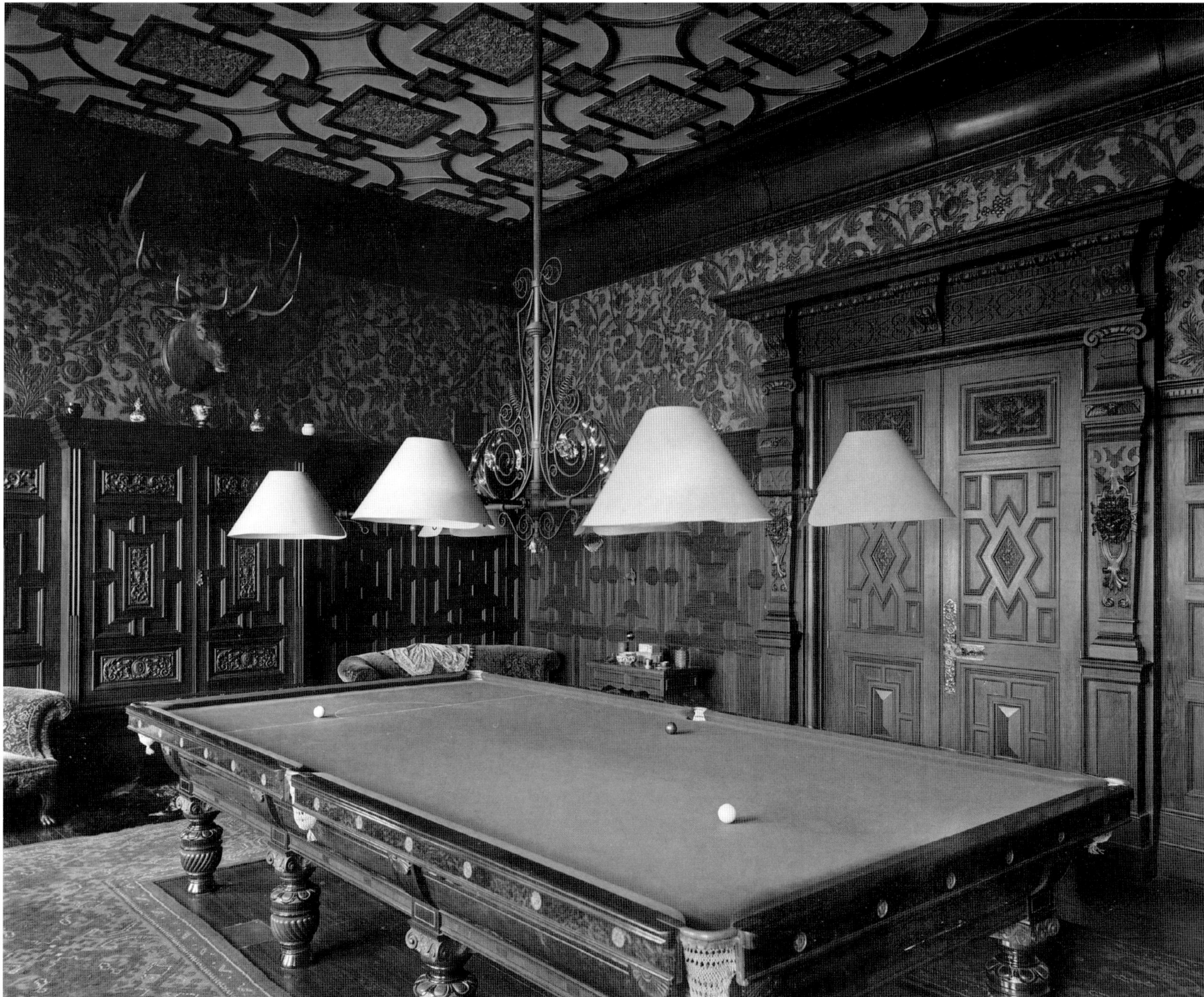

16. The drawing room, Gunavah, Aigburth Drive, October or November 1892 (BL 11874)

This was the home of Ambrose Anthony Vlasto and his wife Anastasia. Both came from families of Greek origin, and Vlasto worked for the Liverpool branch of the Greek merchant house Ralli Brothers. Gunavah was decorated by Turner, Son & Walker. With its inlaid furniture and prayer rug on the wall, the drawing room has a strong flavour of the orient. The exotic highpoint is the tent-like canopy with its luxurious couches and cushions.

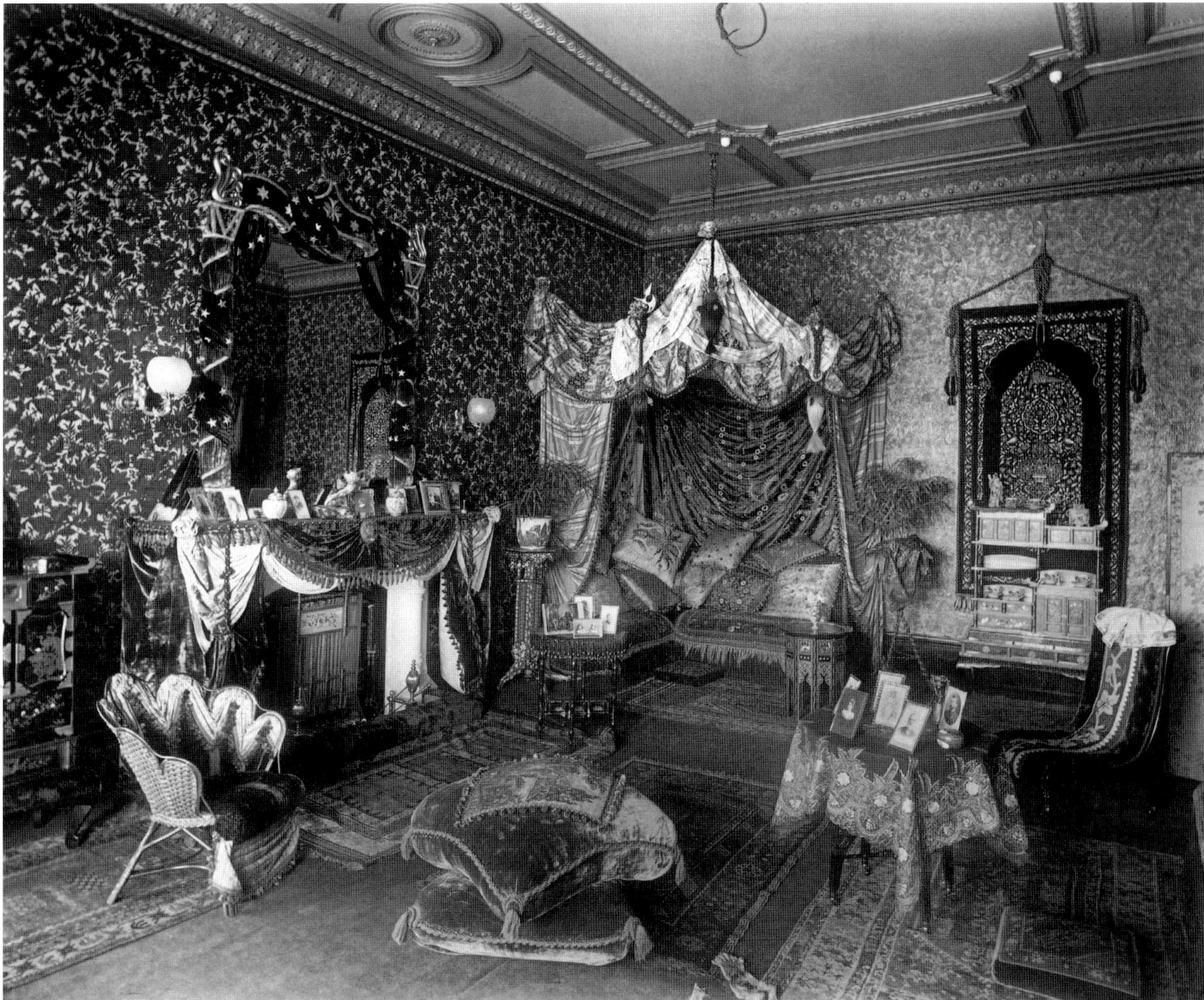

17. The stables, Bidston Court, Vyner Road South, July 1894 (BL 12841/12)

Built for the soap manufacturer Robert Hudson in 1891, Bidston Court was designed by Edward Ould of the Liverpool architects Grayson & Ould. He adopted the style of a traditional Cheshire half-timbered house, modelled on such genuine Tudor examples as Little Moreton Hall. Today only the gatehouse survives in its original location. The mansion itself was dismantled in 1929 and re-erected on a site at Frankby. Its new owner, Sir Ernest Royden, renamed it Hill Bark. It is unusual for Bedford Lemere's photographs to include figures, but this carefully posed image gives an idea of the staff needed to run an establishment the size of Bidston Court. The house can be glimpsed through the archway in the centre, and just visible on the right is the carriage drive leading up to Vyner Road South.

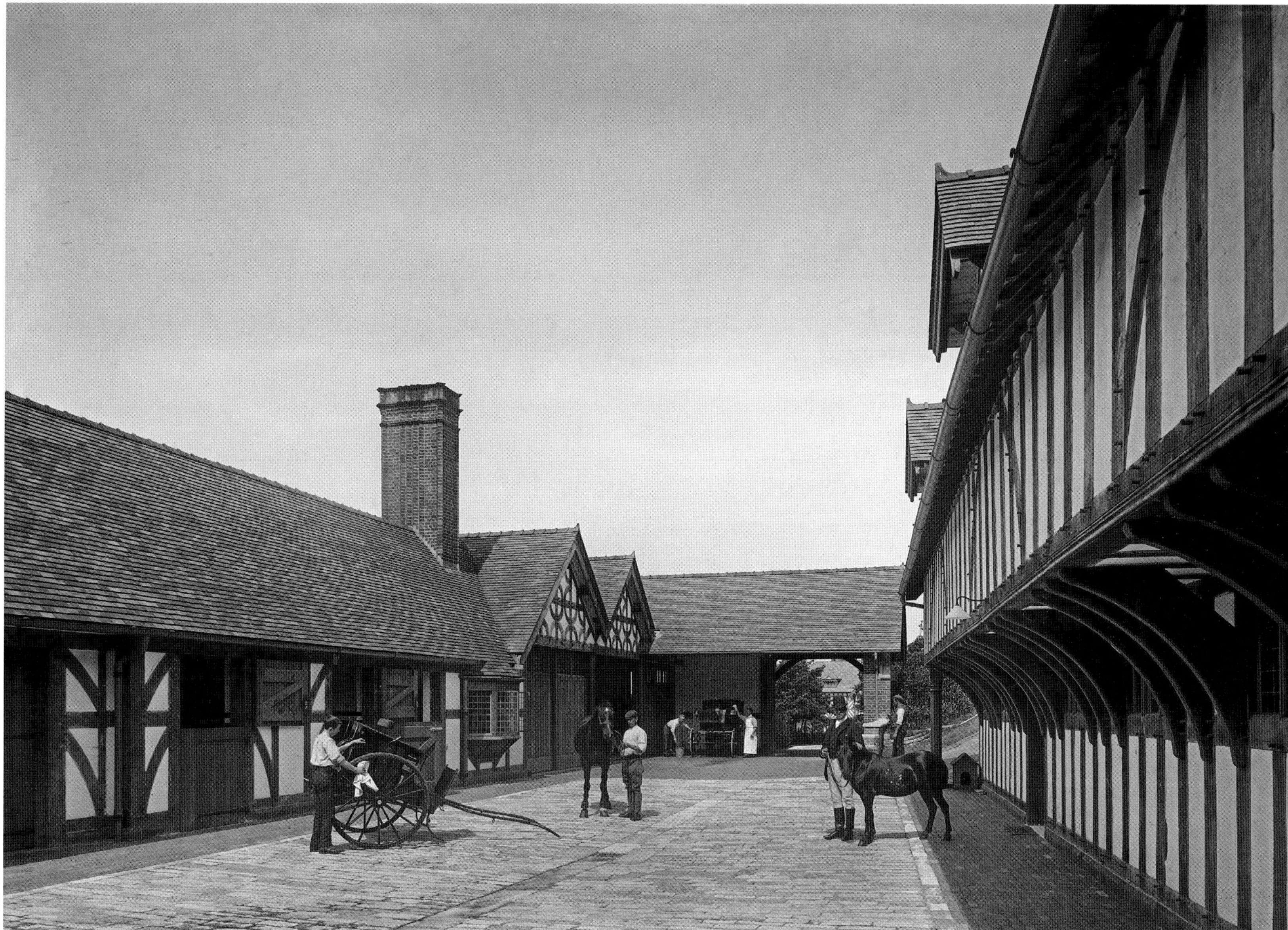

18. The great hall, Bidston Court, July 1894 (BL 12843)

The great halls found in medieval houses were revived by Victorian architects, becoming popular in the last quarter of the nineteenth century. They were used as multi-purpose living rooms – spacious, informal and ideal for entertaining. In the great hall at Bidston Court the stained glass by Morris & Co. shows ancient and modern writers, a theme better suited to a library. At the opposite end, however, was an organ gallery, carved with a quotation from *Romeo and Juliet* suggesting that the room was meant for dancing: 'A hall, a hall! give room! and foot it, girls. More light, you knaves; and turn the tables up.'

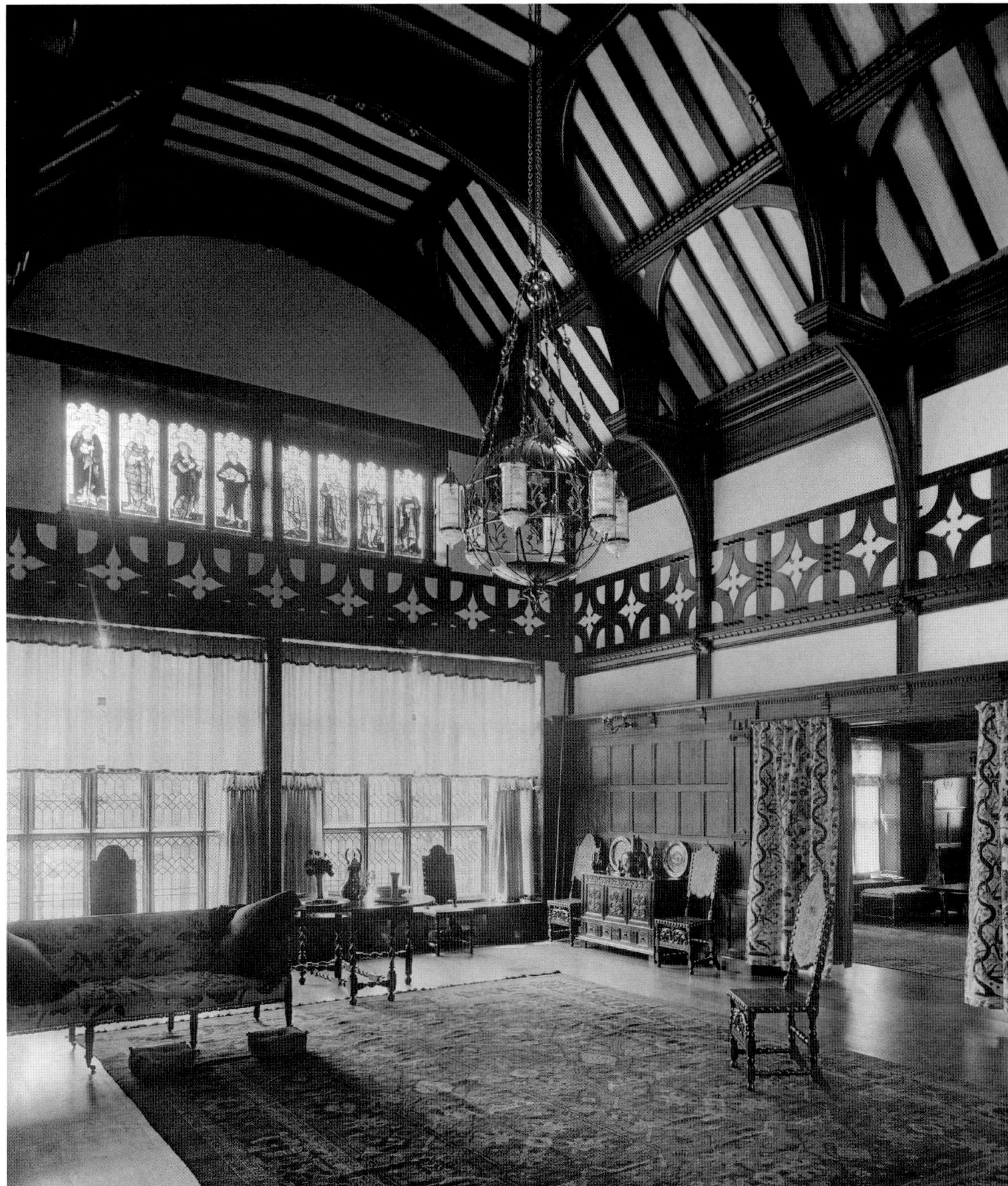

19. The drawing room, Bidston Court, July 1894 (BL 12849)

This room illustrates the range of stylistic influences that fed into the Aesthetic movement of the late nineteenth century: Gothic windows, Tudor plasterwork, Georgian joinery and oriental ceramics. The emphasis is on beauty rather than comfort or relaxation, as the shape of the settees makes clear.

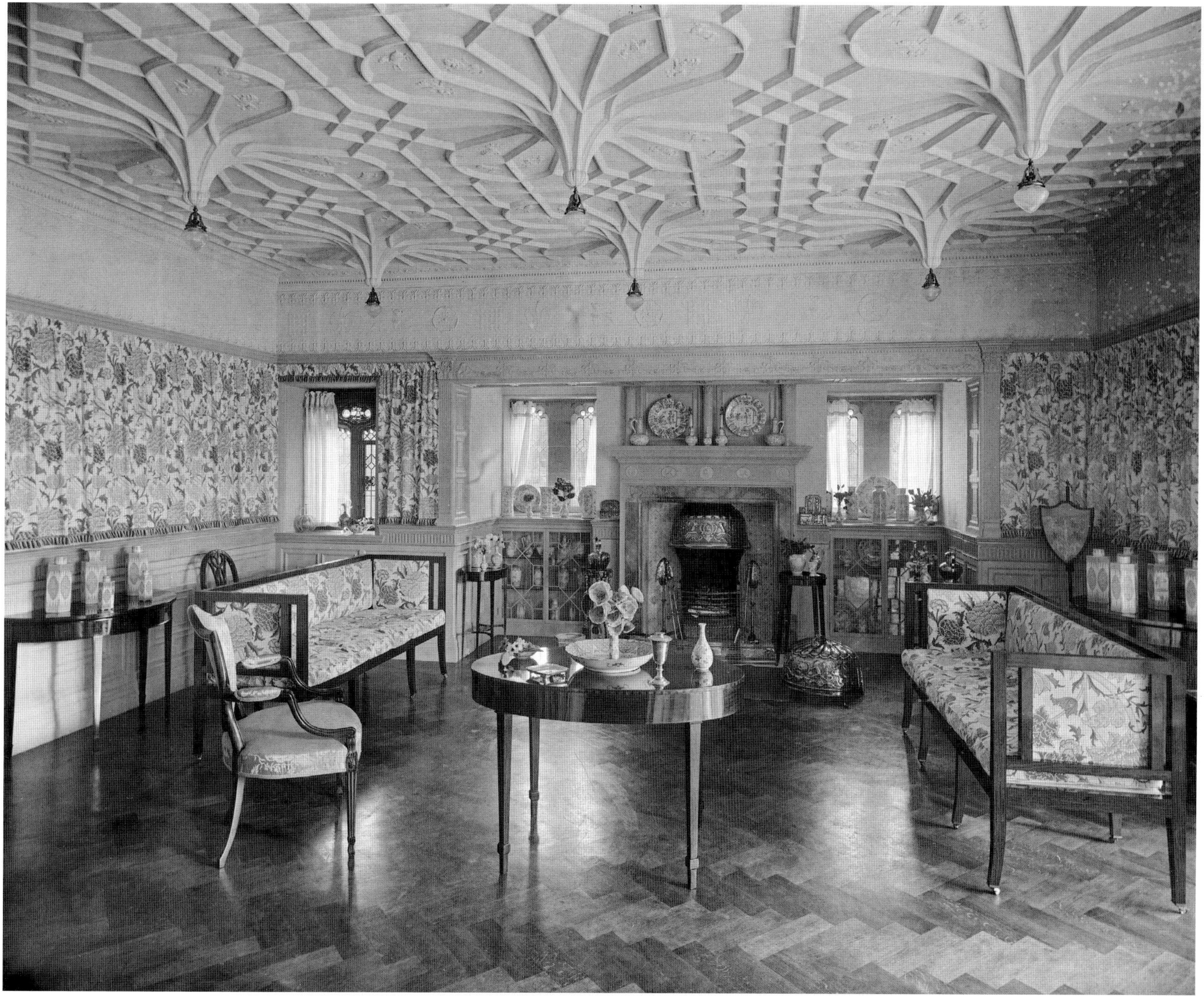

20. The smoking room, Bidston Court, July 1894 (BL 12852)

Despite the spread of the telephone from the 1880s, there is not much evidence that Liverpool's Victorian businessmen worked from home. Unusually, Robert Hudson's smoking room looks like a place for serious work, with its bookshelves and large, well-ordered desk.

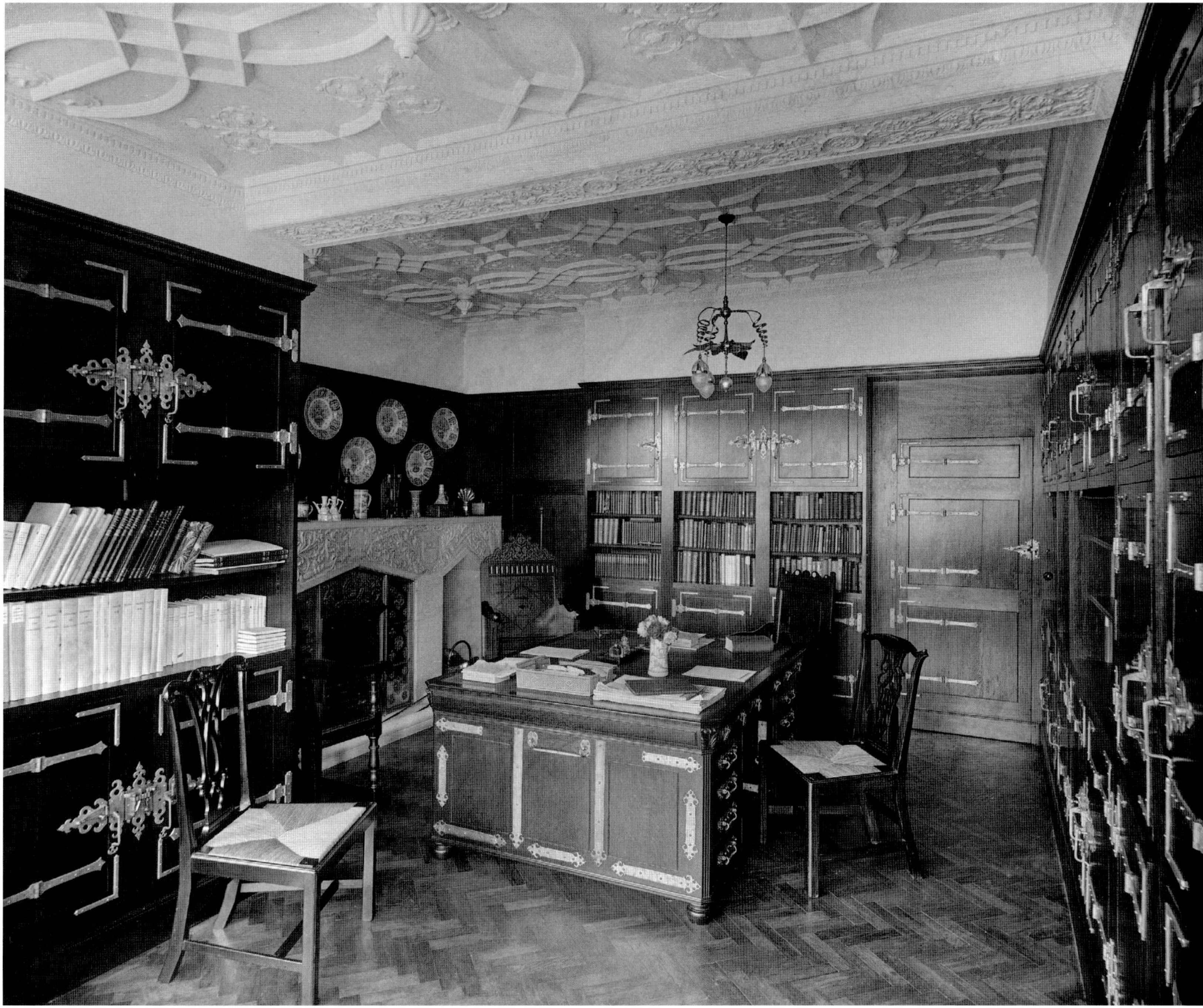

21. The boudoir, Norris Green, West Derby, March 1895 (BL 13045)

Norris Green was built in 1830. For many years, until his death in 1877, it was the home of the extremely wealthy banker John Pemberton Heywood, who married Anna Maria Jones of nearby Lark Hill. In 1894 the contents of the house were auctioned, and when Arthur Heywood Jones of Lark Hill went to live there with his wife the following year, it was furnished for them by Turner, Son & Walker. To create this boudoir a simple early-nineteenth-century room was overlaid with a variety of decorative furniture and fittings, including a Rococo chimneypiece. The delicate chairs and the pictures of courtship on the end wall identify it as a female preserve.

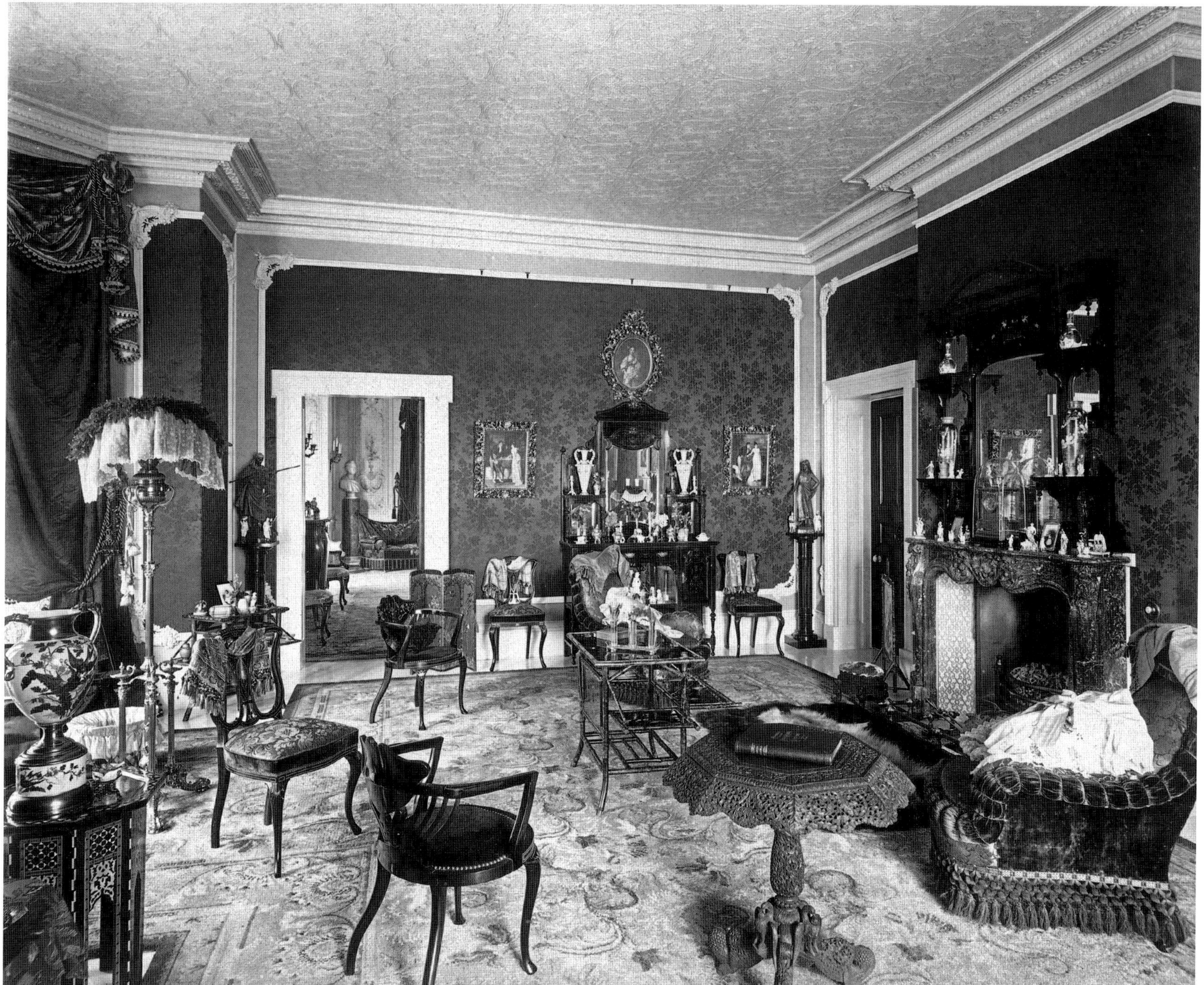

22. The smoking room, Norris Green, March 1895 (BL 13055)

Every surface in this extraordinary room is decorated with a different pattern. Embossed paper, usually reserved for friezes or dados, here fills the whole space between skirting and cornice. The pictures featuring dogs and horses reflect Arthur Heywood Jones's interests – he was a successful owner of greyhounds – and in contrast to the ladies' boudoir (plate 21) the whole room has a heavy, masculine character. A late winter fire is burning in the grate.

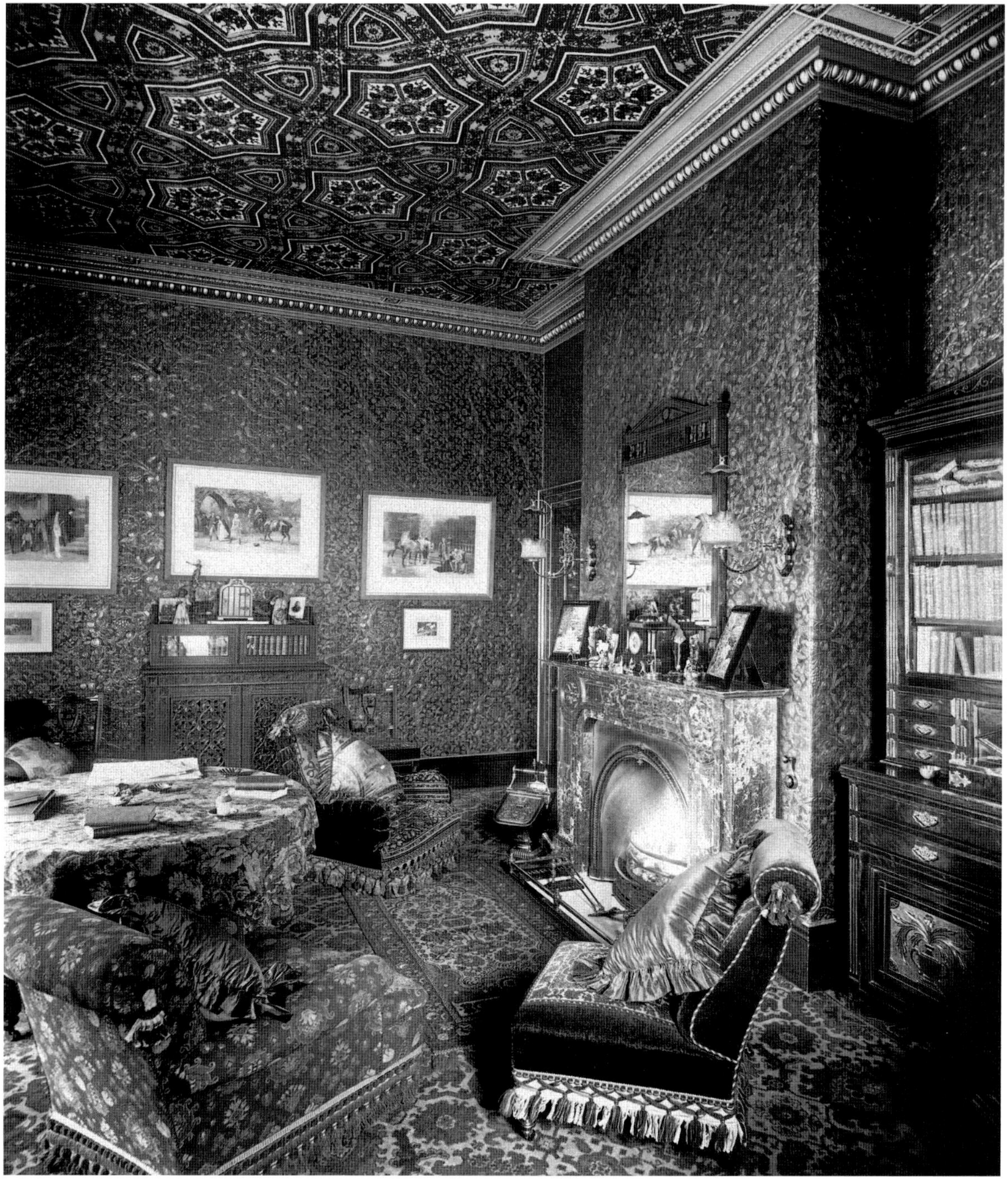

23. **Dawpool, Thurstaston, 1896** (BL 13481/8)

Thomas Henry Ismay, chairman of the White Star Line, and his wife Margaret moved into this grand new house overlooking the Dee estuary in 1884. It was designed for them by Richard Norman Shaw, who was later responsible for the White Star Line offices in James Street, Liverpool. The Liverpool architect J. Francis Doyle worked with him on both commissions. Margaret Ismay's diaries show that she and her husband were closely involved in the design and furnishing of Dawpool. They visited other houses to gather ideas, shopped together for antique furniture, and deliberated with the decorator J. Aldam Heaton over the treatment of the interior.

T.H. Ismay died in 1899, Margaret Ismay in 1907, and afterwards their children chose to live elsewhere. 'Poor old Dawpool', wrote Shaw. 'Perhaps it can be turned into a sanatorium or a smallpox hospital! I remember Mrs Ismay saying to me more than 10 years ago, that even then it had more than answered its purpose, for it had interested and amused Mr Ismay every day of his life for 15 years!' (Shaw to Frederick Radcliffe, 30 November 1907, quoted in Andrew Saint, 'Norman Shaw's letters: a selection', *Architectural History*, 18, 1975). The house was eventually demolished in 1927.

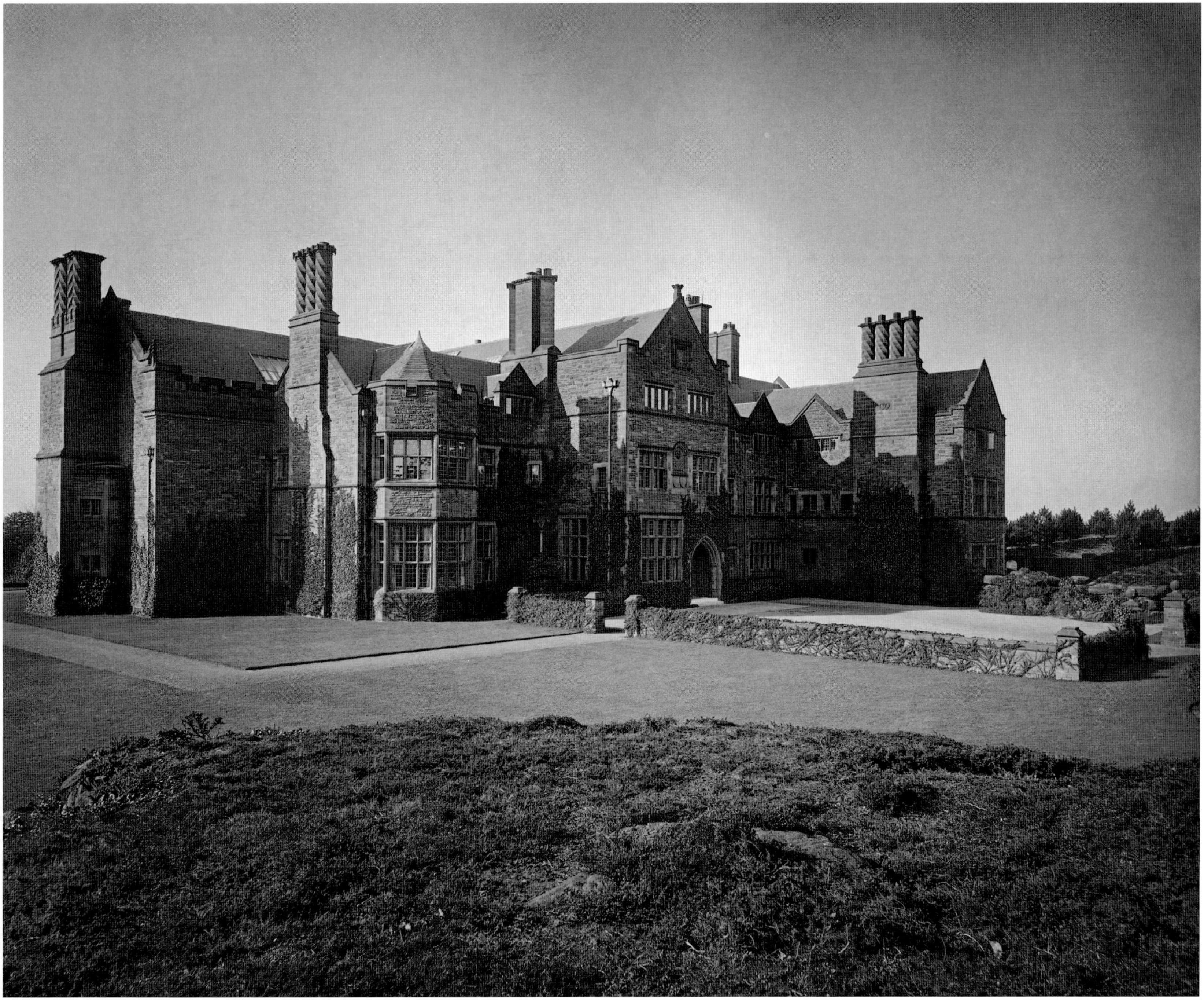

24. The picture room, Dawpool, 1896 (BL 13484)

This was the largest room at Dawpool and served as a gallery for T.H. Ismay's art collection. On the easel is Rossetti's *The Loving Cup*. The house was lit by electricity from the start, so that here the natural light from the glazed ceiling could be supplemented by electroliers. When the house was demolished, the upper part of the spectacular chimneypiece was removed to the village of Portmeirion in North Wales, where it was eventually incorporated into the domed building known as the Pantheon. The lower part was taken by T.H. Ismay's son James and reused at Iwerne Minster House in Dorset.

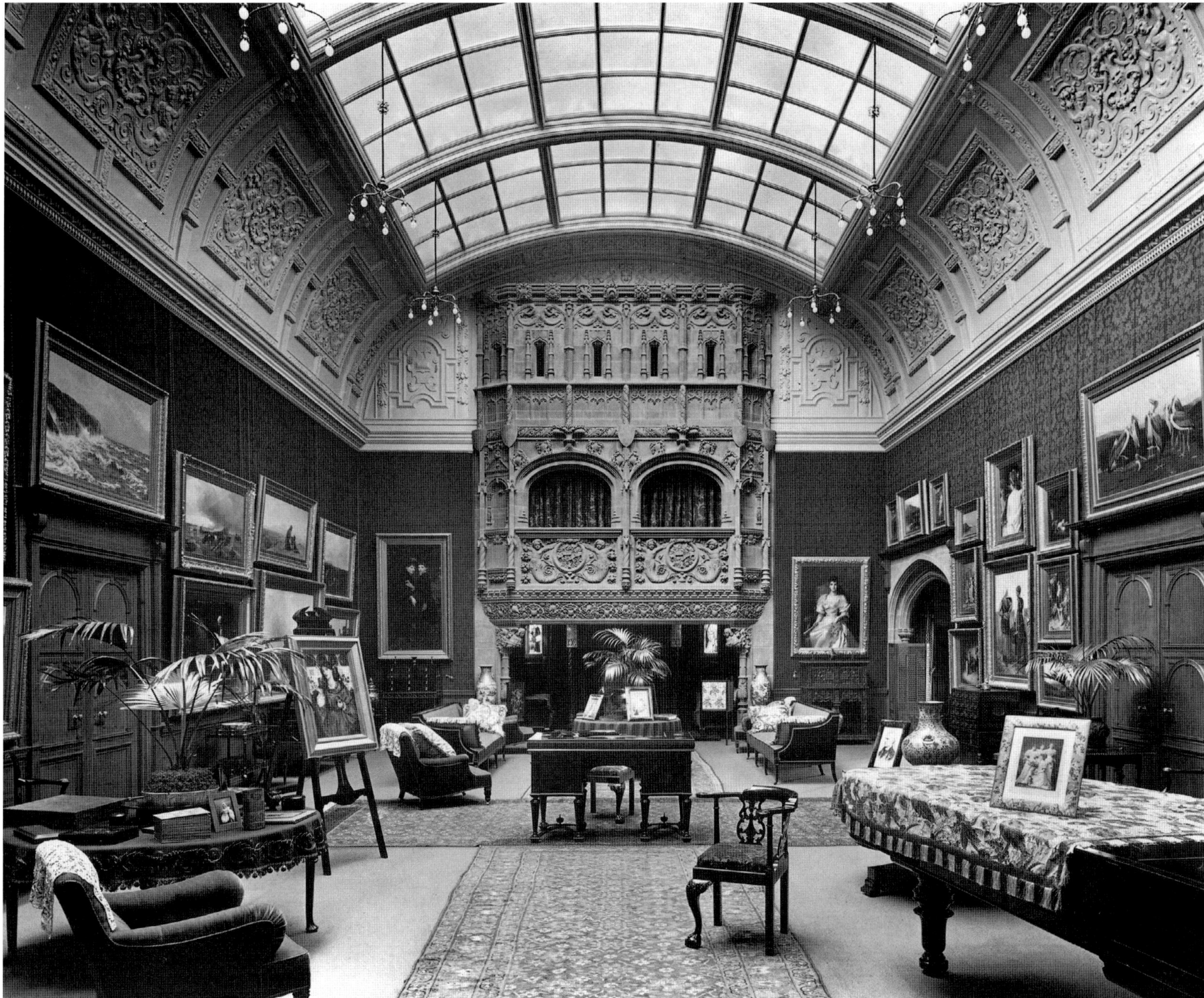

25. The dining room fireplace, Dawpool, 1896 (BL 13488)

This colossal fireplace was removed when Dawpool was demolished. It was reused as the entrance to what is now the Kingsland Cabaret Restaurant, at the corner of Borough Road and Kingsland Road in Birkenhead, where it still remains.

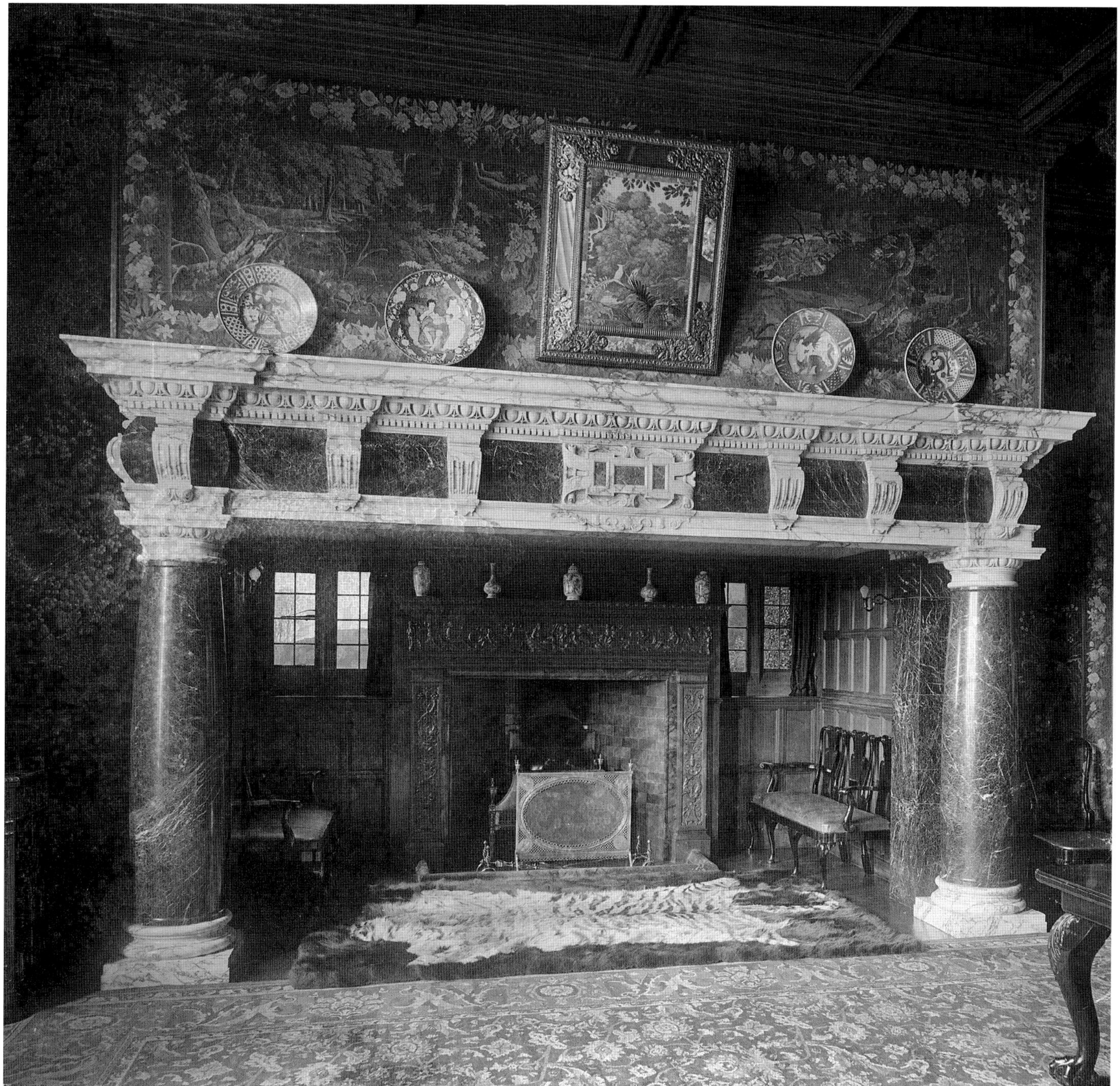

26. The conservatory, Palmyra, Aigburth Vale, 1896 (BL 13554)

Palmyra was the home of S.J. Waring, furnisher and decorator. It was a simple early-nineteenth-century villa with later additions, including this ambitious octagonal-roofed conservatory leading to a sequence of interconnecting glasshouses. The full-length mirror framed in the arch on the left would have made the space seem even larger.

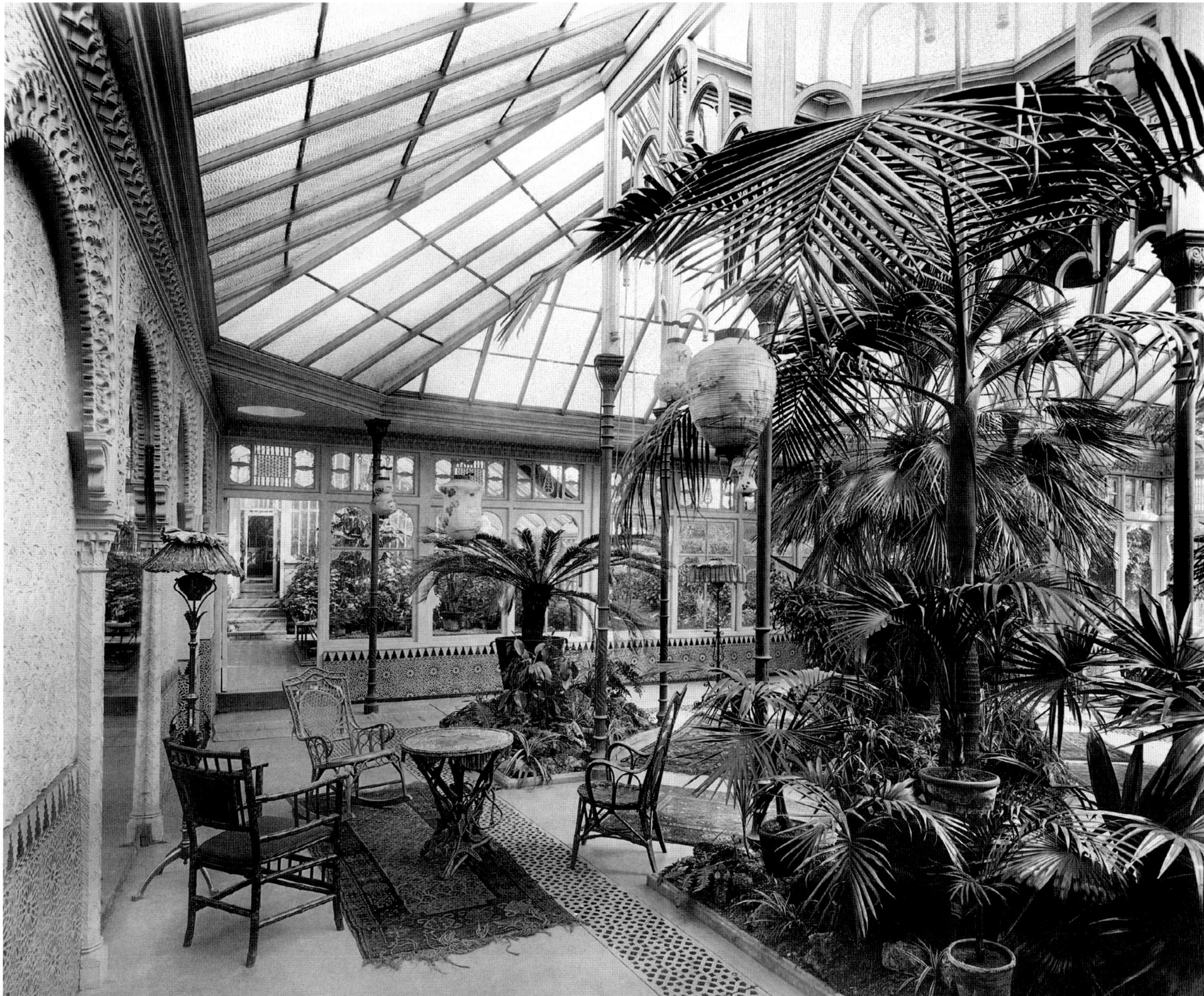

27. The dining room, Enmore, 34 Alexandra Drive, 5 August 1896 (BL 13773)

Richard R. Lockett completed this dining room extension in 1896, the date carved above the portrait over the fireplace. With its panelling, plasterwork and big oriel window it looks like part of an Elizabethan manor house. The coats of arms on the chimneypiece show Lockett's pride in his ancestry, but the very lavishness of this heraldic display suggests a man who felt insecure about his social status.

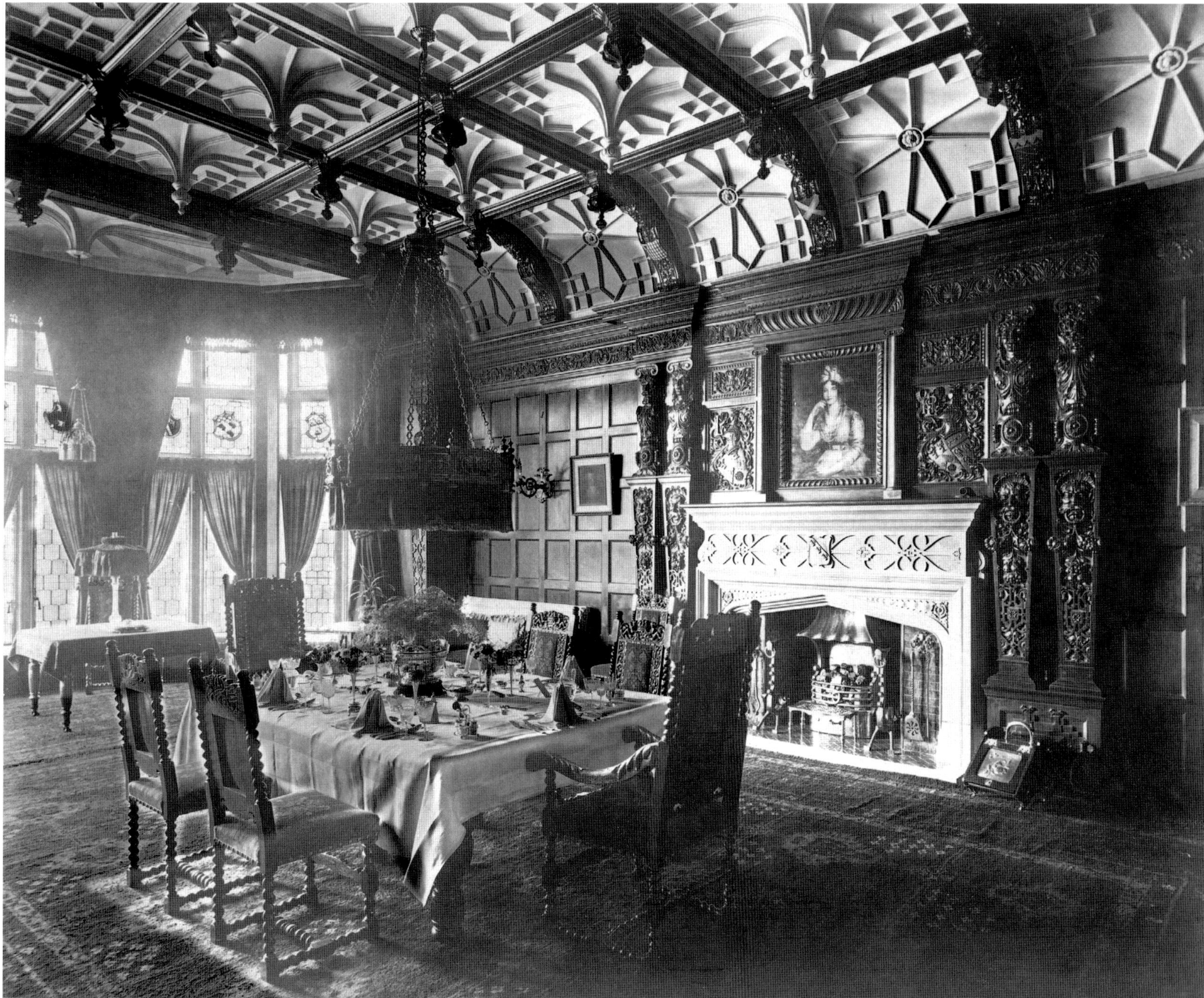

28. The drawing room, Enmore, 5 August 1896 (BL 13775)

In contrast to the dining room, the drawing room at Enmore was decorated in French Rococo style.

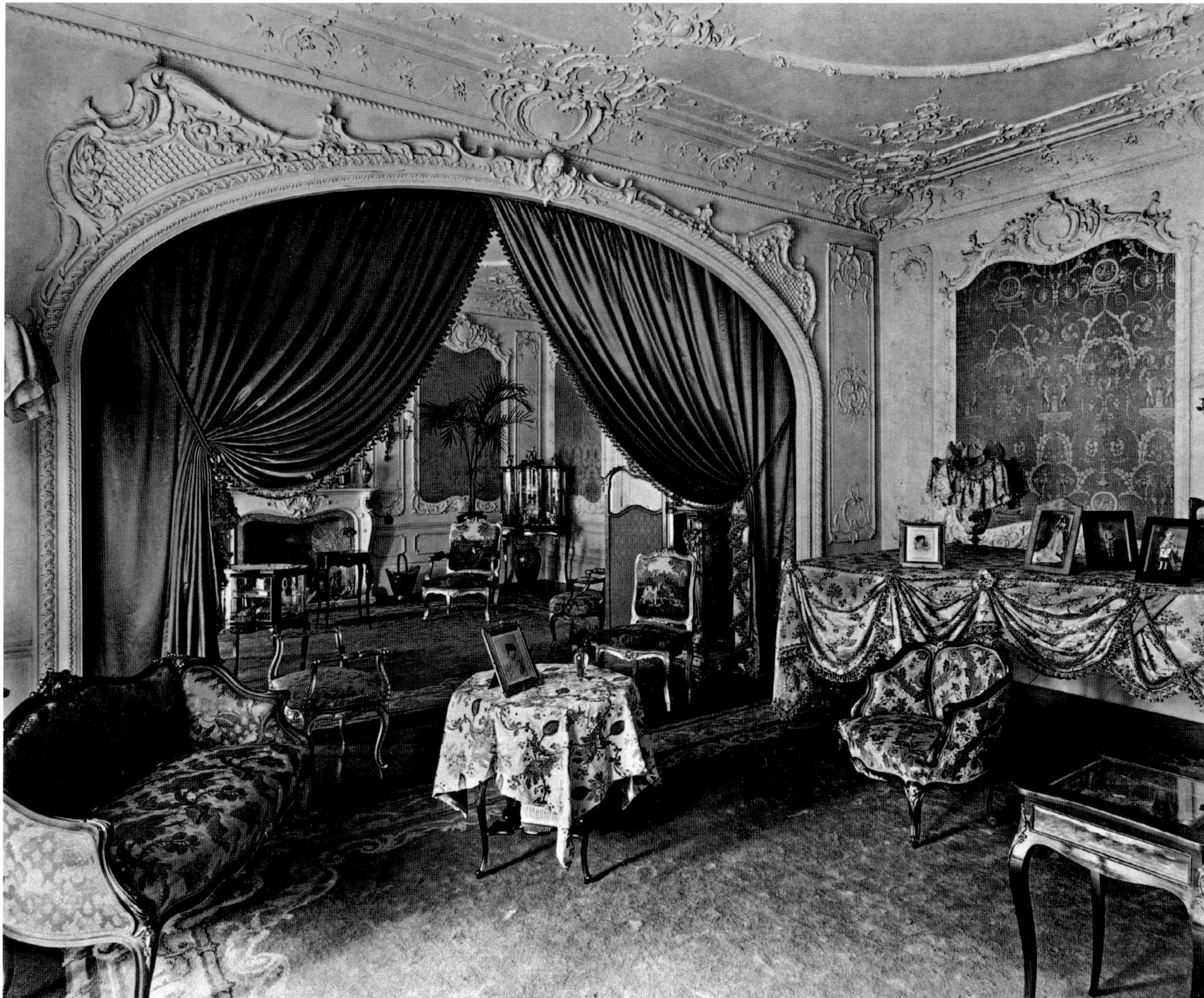

29. The hall, 4 Croxteth Drive, 1900 (BL 15771)

This was the home of William Nelson, founder of the Nelson Line of steamers. In the 1880s he was a pioneer in the use of refrigerated ships to import frozen meat from Argentina. He moved from Old Swan to this more prestigious address around 1898-9, and had the house redecorated by G.H. Morton & Son.

The spacious hall and grand staircase were obviously meant to impress visitors with a sense of Nelson's social standing: the stag's head above the fireplace suggests an aristocratic country house rather than a large suburban villa. In due course Nelson moved to a real country house – Acton Park near Wrexham – and was made a baronet. The large painting under the stairs is *A Hunted Jewess, France, 1610* by Ellen Clacy, shown in the 1889 Liverpool Autumn Exhibition at the Walker Art Gallery. On the pilaster to the left of this is a display of Maori weapons: with their worldwide trading links, Liverpool merchants and shipowners were well placed to collect 'exotic' artefacts such as these.

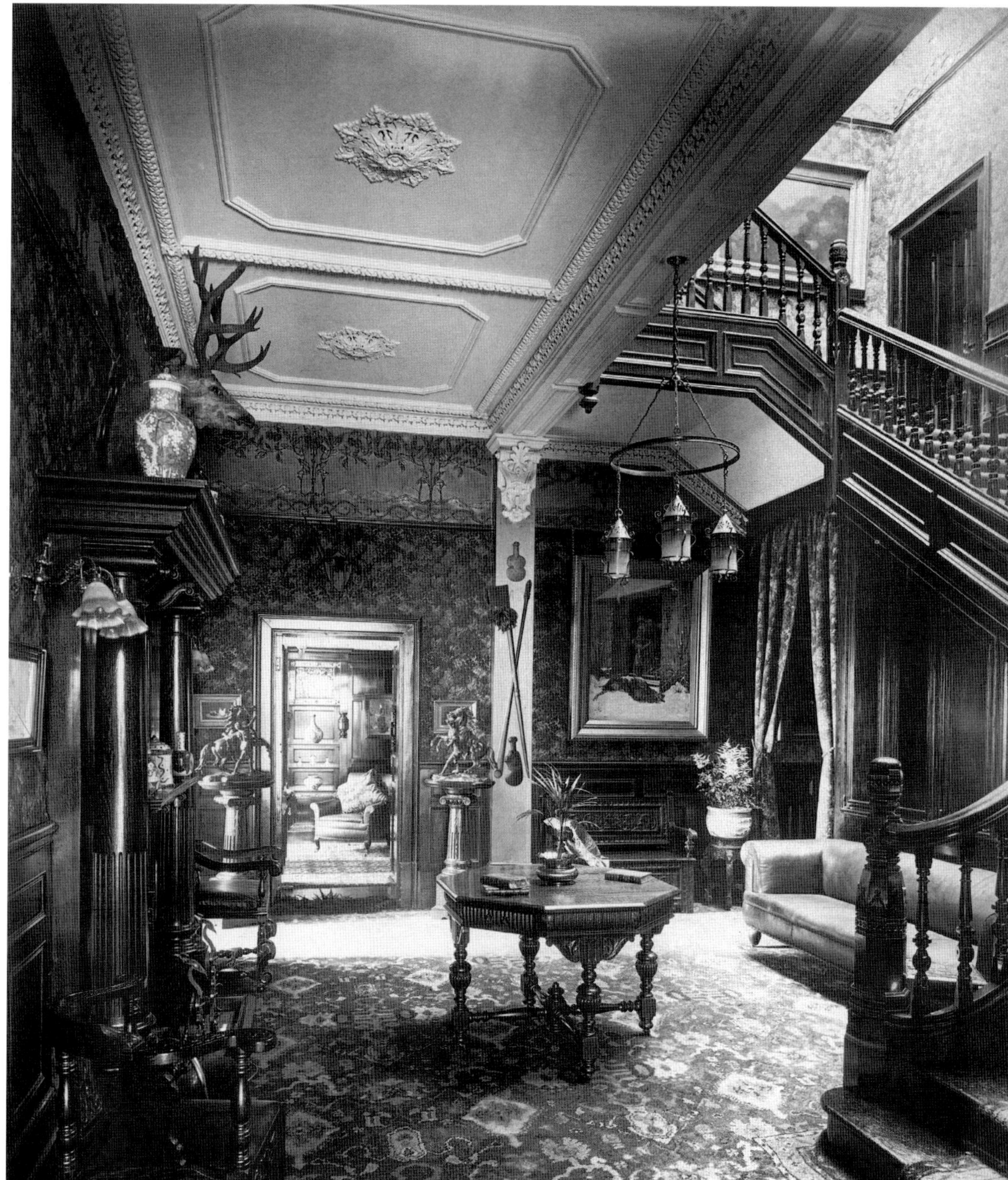

30. The dining room, 4 Croxteth Drive, 1900 (BL 15775)

The inscription on the sideboard – 'Who carves, is kind to two; who talks, to all' – is a quotation from the seventeenth-century poet George Herbert. In this context (though not in the original poem) it celebrates convivial eating. It also hints at the fact that William Nelson was a successful meat importer and cattle merchant. His initial 'N' is stamped on the leather backs of the chairs. The door used by family and guests is on the left; the door leading to the kitchen is hidden behind the screen on the right.

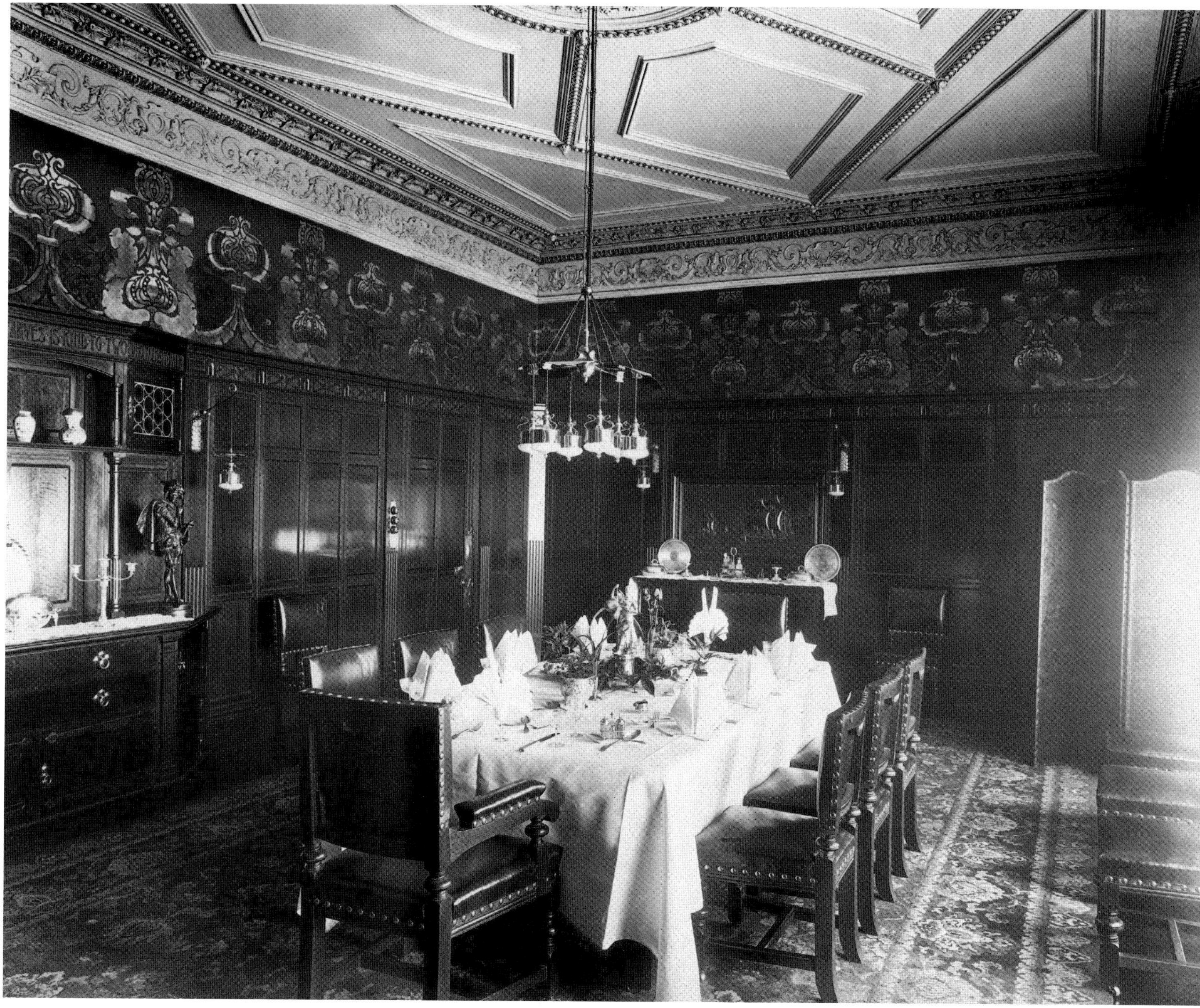

31. Drawing room fireplace, Sefton House, Ullet Road, 1900 (BL 16129)

Sefton House was the home of the shipping magnate Dashper Edward Glynn. In 1900 he employed Edmund Rathbone and the Bromsgrove Guild to carry out a scheme of decoration illustrating the story of the water spirit Undine. The frieze of fish and mermaids and the figures on the mantelshelf – representing Undine and her grieving foster parents – are by the sculptor Benjamin Creswick. The watery theme of the story made it doubly suitable for Glynn, a shipowner whose favourite pastime was salmon fishing.

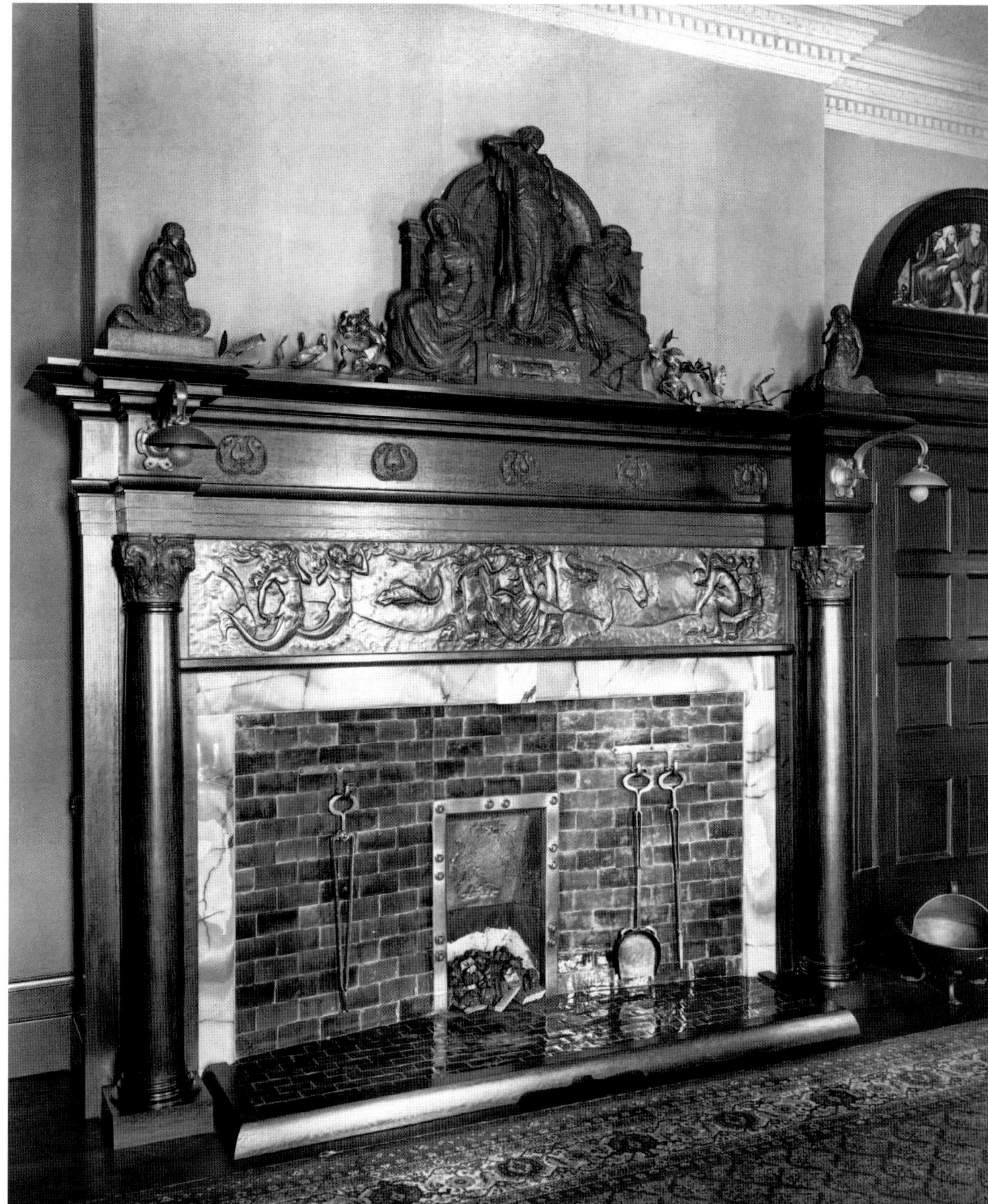

32. The music room, Holmestead, North Mossley Hill Road, July 1901 (BL 16685)

At this date Holmestead was occupied by the retired shipowner and art collector William Imrie. Dominating the music room is Edward Burne-Jones's painting *The Tree of Forgiveness*. After Imrie's death it was acquired by W.H. Lever and is now in the Lady Lever Art Gallery. The large picture to the left of the fireplace is *Why Seek Ye the Living Amongst the Dead?* by Spencer Stanhope, now in the Art Gallery of New South Wales. The sculpture in the window recess seems to be a version of John Henry Foley's *Winter*. The wallpaper is William Morris's 'Acanthus' pattern, designed in 1875.

Domestic music parties were important social occasions for Liverpool's Victorian elite, and professional performers were sometimes employed. The chemical manufacturer Andrew Kurtz attended a concert at Holmestead in 1882, featuring opera singers who had recently performed at the Alexandra Theatre in Lime Street. 'One or two of the men had fine voices', he noted in his diary, but 'the prima donna's voice was in a state of rapid decay' *(Liverpool Libraries, Liverpool Record Office: 920 KUR 1/22, diary of A.G. Kurtz, 10 March 1882).*

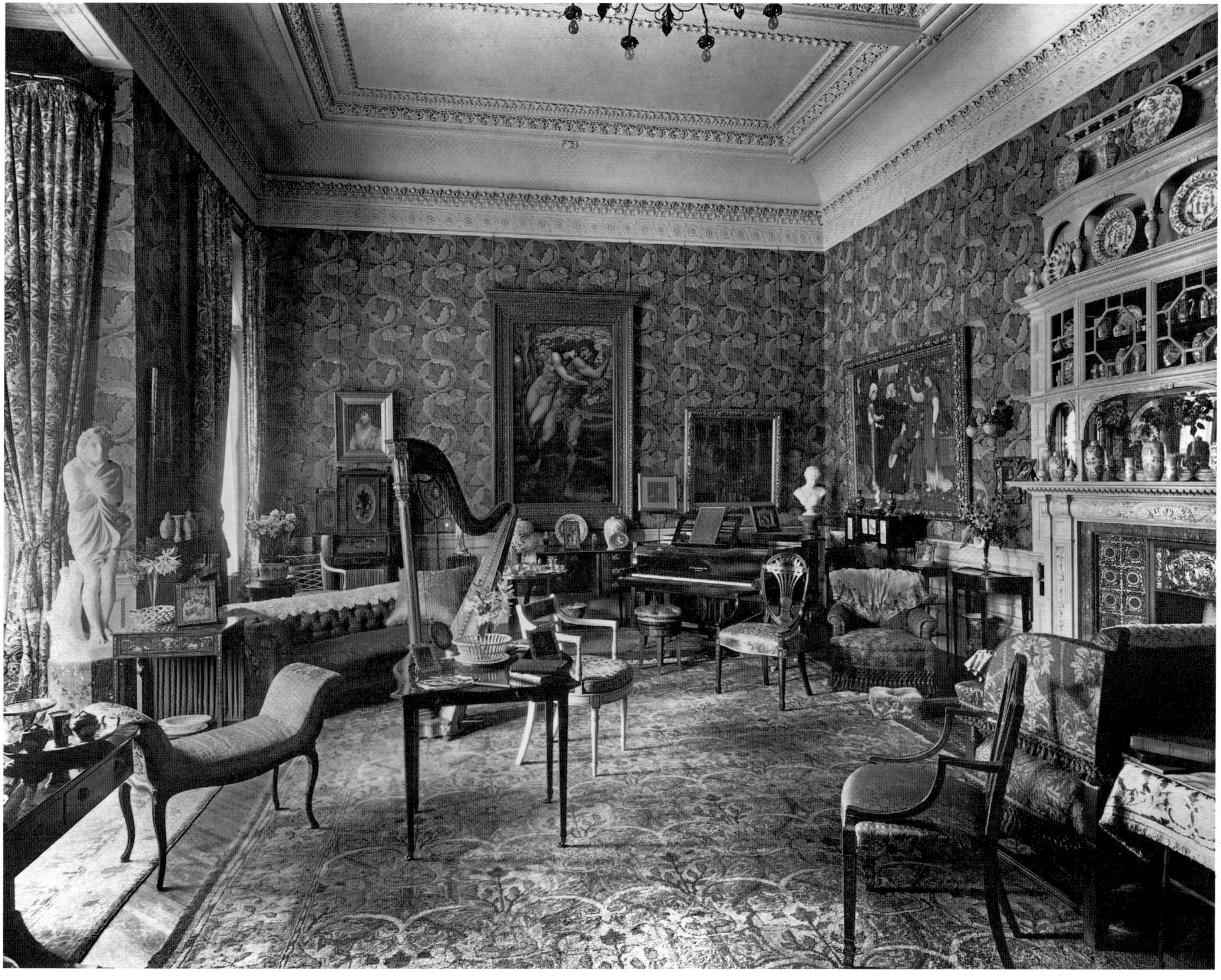

33. The library, Holmestead, July 1901 (BL 16690)

William Imrie was the most important patron of the late Pre-Raphaelite and Symbolist artist Evelyn de Morgan. Her painting *The Dryad* hangs to the right of the window and her *Gloria in Excelsis* is in pride of place above the fireplace. Between them is a reduced version of *Dante's Dream* by Rossetti, one of two that Imrie owned; the original full-size painting is in the Walker Art Gallery. The stained glass window of 1895 is by Morris & Co., and shows St Cecilia, patron saint of music.

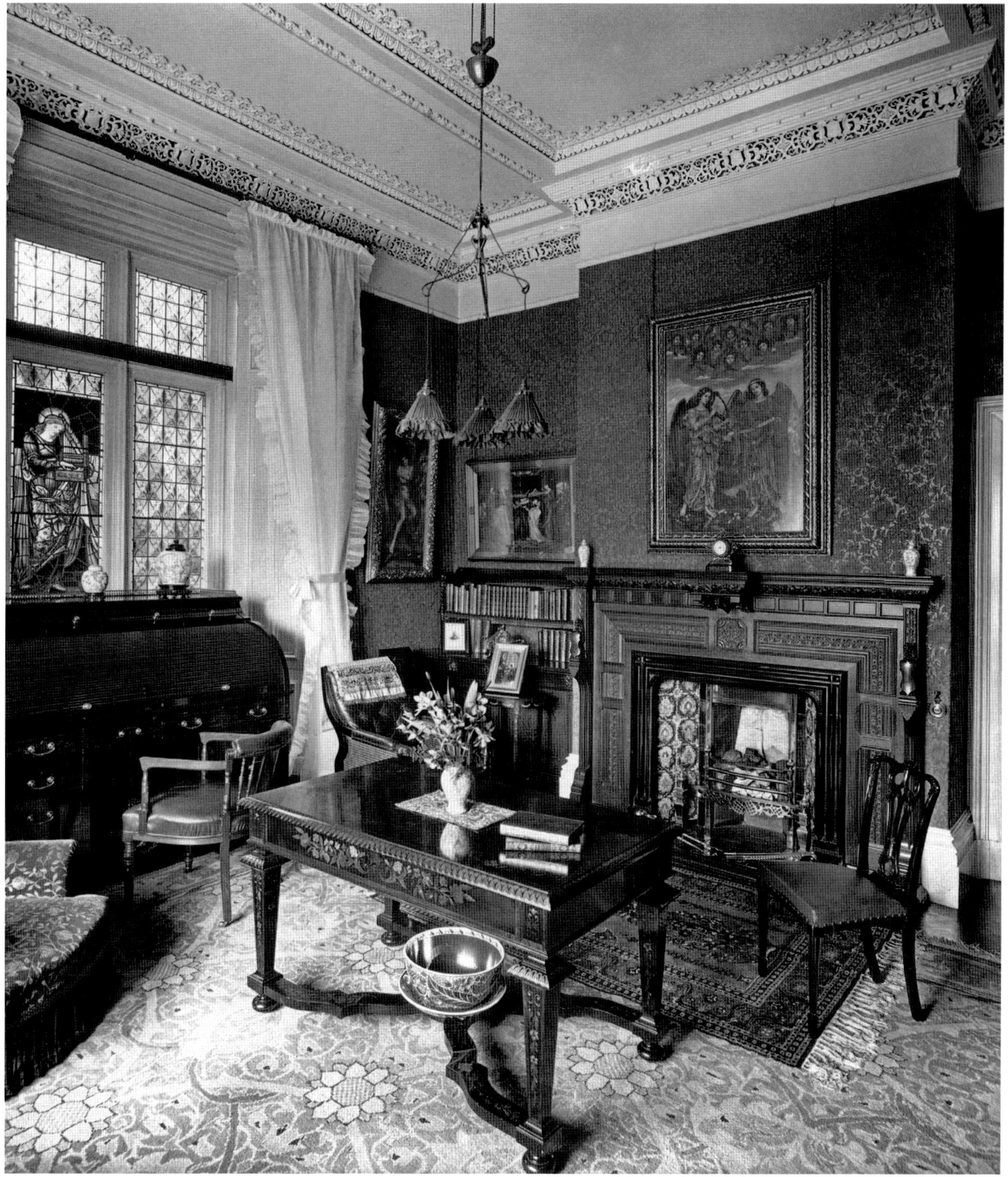

34. The billiard room, Holmestead, July 1901 (BL 16697)

The builder Samuel Holme erected Holmestead for himself in the 1840s. The original Gothic villa was doubled in size in 1869-70 by a new owner, the cotton broker Michael Belcher, whose additions included this billiard room: his initials are carved on the fireplace, and on the corbel above and to the right of the door. Billiards provided an important opportunity for businessmen to socialise. In Liverpool, most large houses built in the second half of the nineteenth century included a purpose-designed billiard room, while older houses would often have one added or converted from an existing room. According to one of his obituaries, the quiet, retiring William Imrie had to be persuaded to install a billiard table when he bought Holmestead in 1883, but 'in after years he became somewhat devoted to the game as a gentle recreation' (*Journal of Commerce*, 8 August 1906). On the right of the door is what appears to be an automatic piano or organ, and a cabinet containing the music rolls needed to play it. The painting over the fireplace – *Nelson Capturing a Spanish Ship at the Battle of St Vincent* by F. Baden-Powell – is now in the Walker Art Gallery.

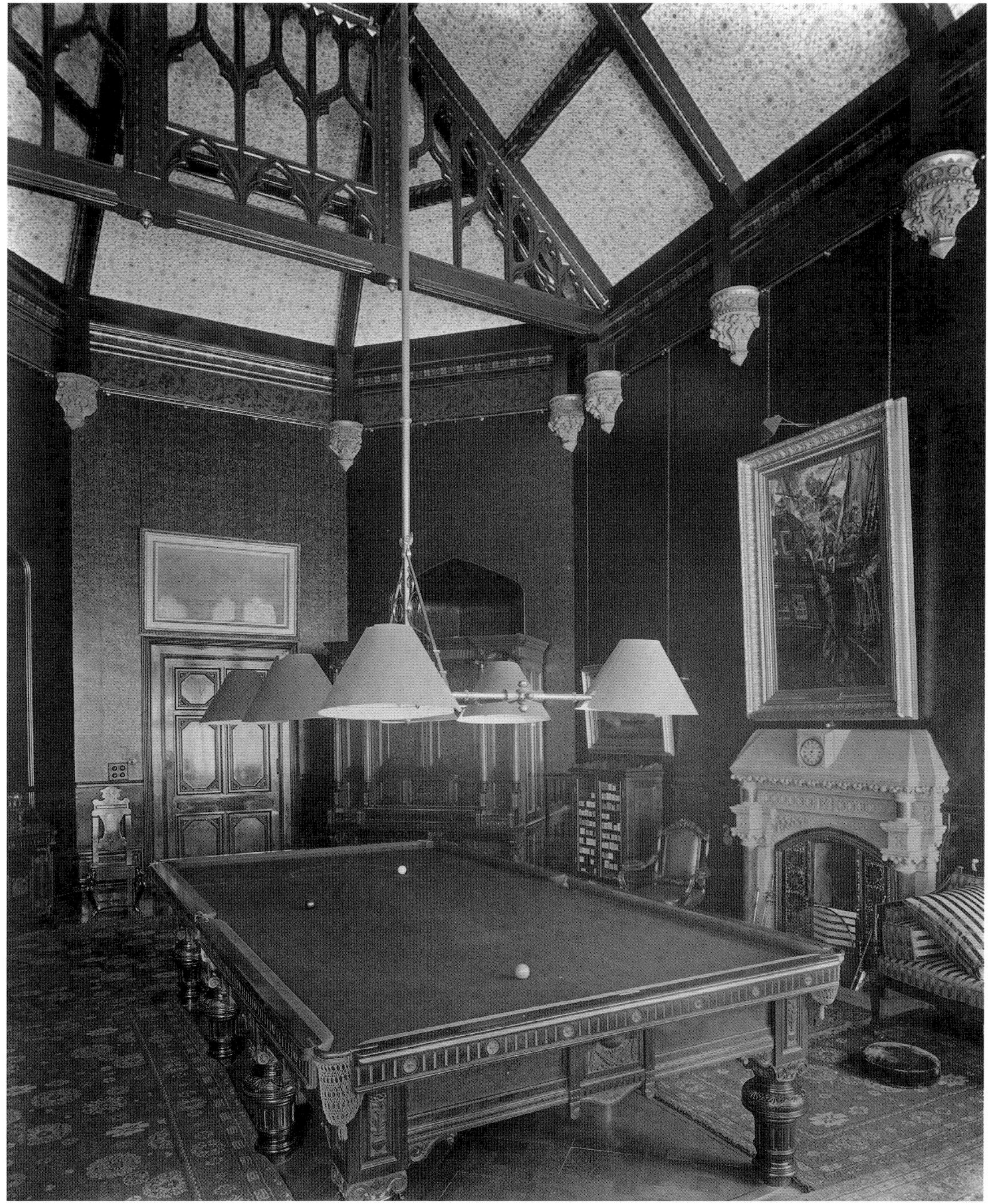

35. The library, Sandamona, Talbot Road, Noctorum, 1902 (BL 16951)

The home of Alexander Charles Ziegler, cotton merchant and partner in the firm of Merrifield, Ziegler & Co. The house was designed by J.J. Talbot. The library is furnished in a comfortable, understated eighteenth-century style – very different from the opulence of Talbot's contemporary music room for W.H. Lever at Thornton Manor (see plate 37).

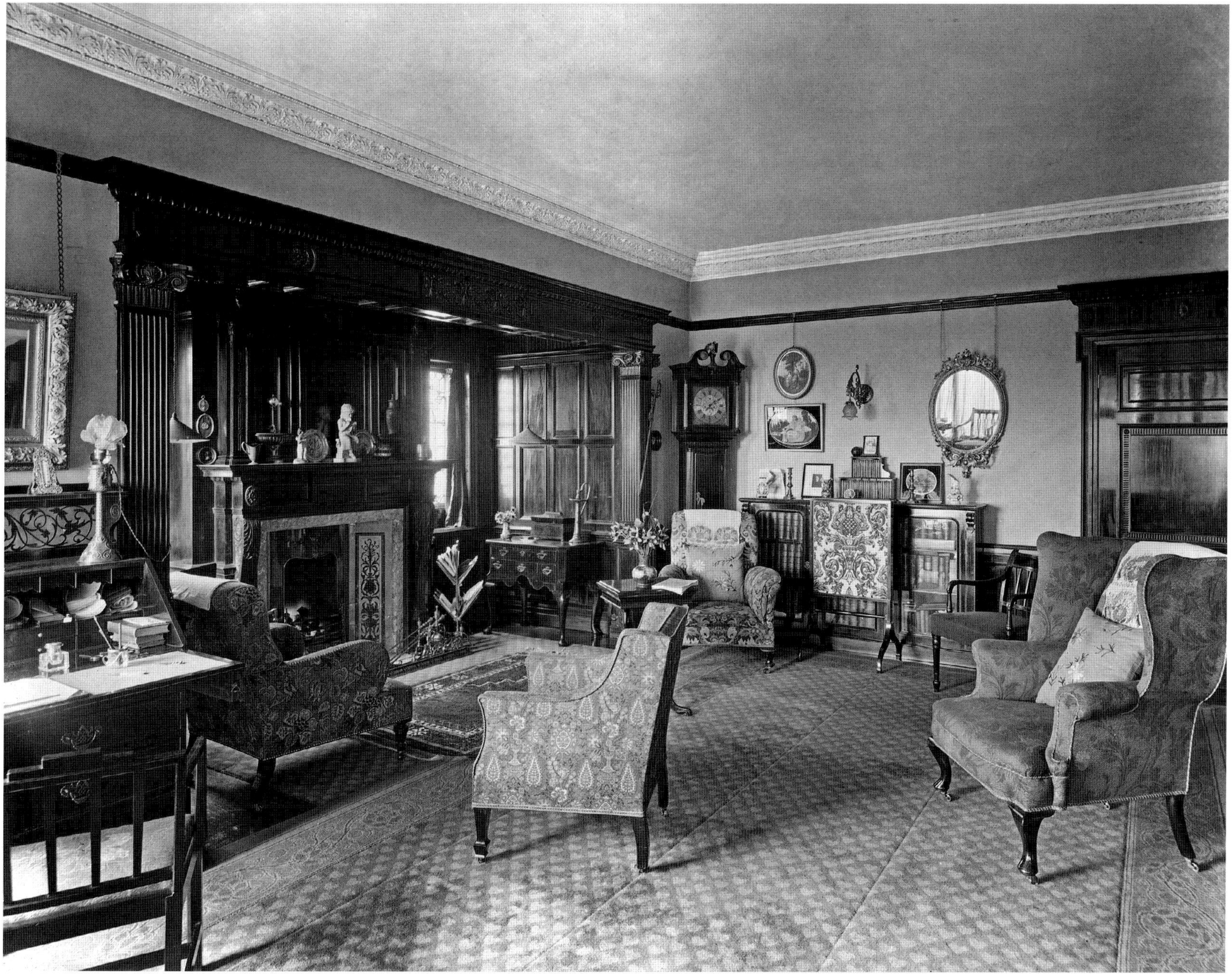

36. The music room, Marlfield, West Derby, 1903 (BL 17541)

Marlfield was the home of Richard le Doux. Born in Germany, he moved to Liverpool in 1868 and became director of a company supplying antifouling paint for ships' hulls. He was a friend and patron of the Croatian artist Vlaho Bukovac, whose paintings appear in this photograph. Some aspects of this room are quite conventional, but others are more unusual: the stylised floral patterns on the walls and ceiling reflect continental Art Nouveau, while the most eye-catching feature, the curious chandelier, has no obvious precedent. The decorators were Waring & Gillow.

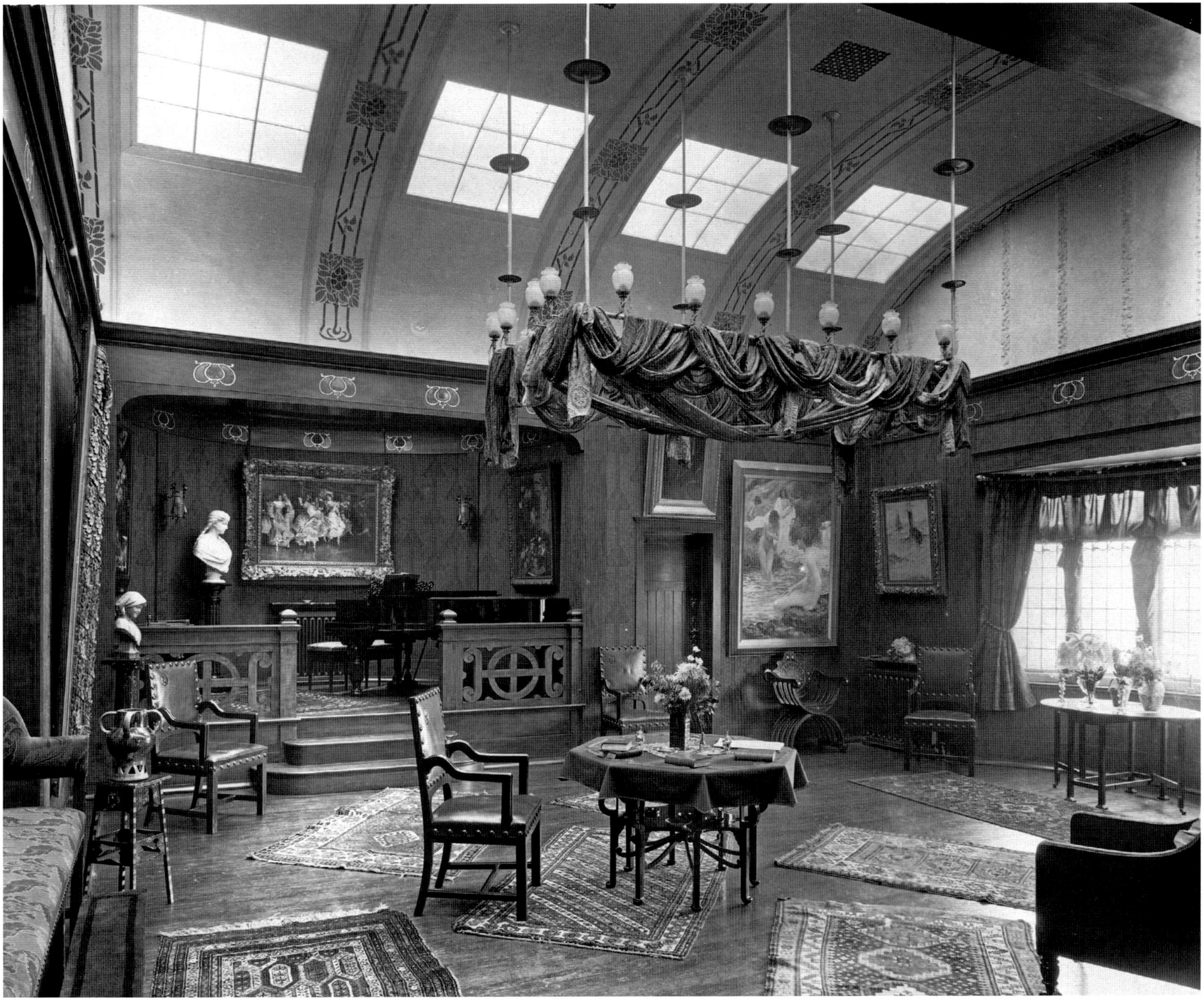

37. The music room, Thornton Manor, 1903 (BL 17551)

In 1888 William Hesketh Lever rented Thornton Manor, a modest early-Victorian villa three miles from Port Sunlight. Over the next twenty-five years he remodelled and extended it, transforming it into a grand country house. The music room of 1902, designed by J.J. Talbot in Renaissance style, was influenced by T.H. Ismay's earlier picture room at Dawpool, both being top-lit to serve as galleries. Several works now in the Lady Lever Art Gallery are visible: on the end wall hang J.E. Millais's *The Black Brunswickers* and Lord Leighton's *Fatidica*, and in front of the latter is Maurice Ferrary's sculpture *Leda and the Swan*.

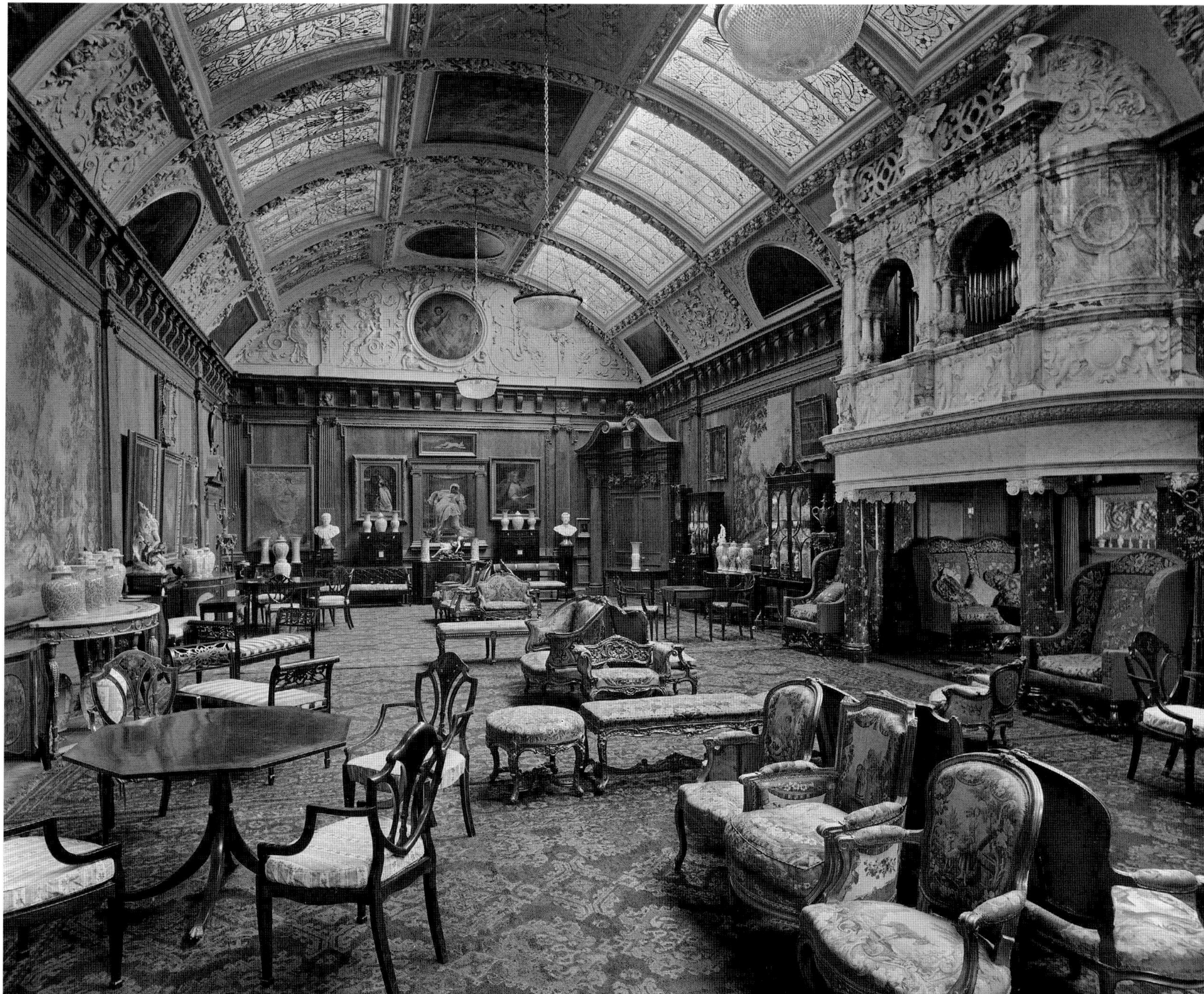

38. The music room, Thornton Manor, 1903 (BL 17555)

Occupying one end of the music room, this shrine-like alcove contains recesses with glass shelves and mirrored backs, in which some of W.H. Lever's Chinese porcelain is displayed. In 1902 he was said to have one of the finest such collections in Europe. Flanking the alcove are two busts by Edward Onslow Ford which had special significance for Lever: on the right, his father; on the left, the Liberal statesman W.E. Gladstone who was his political hero. Both are now in the Lady Lever Art Gallery.

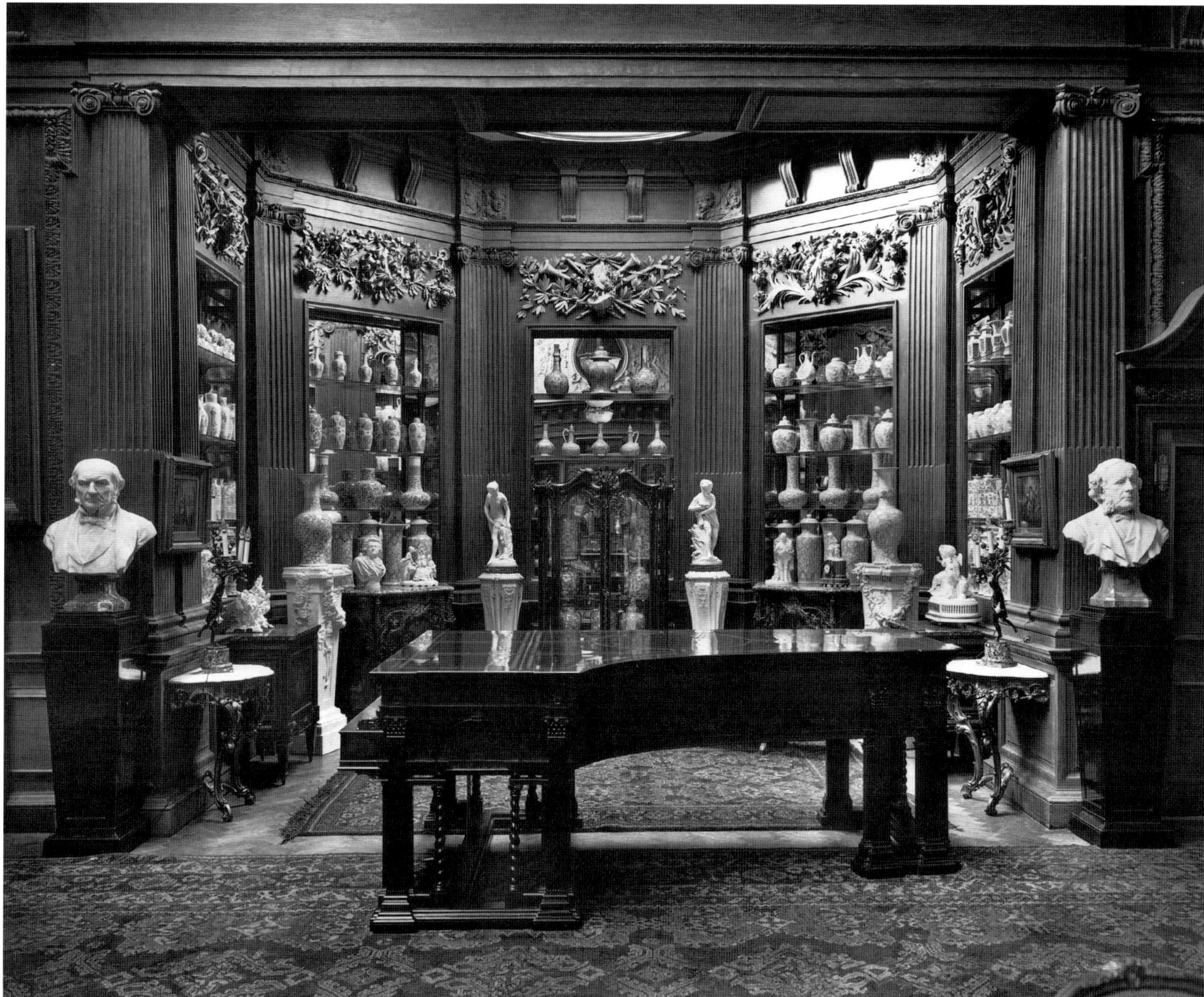

39. Gledhill, Mossley Hill Drive, Sefton Park, April 1904 (BL 18181)

Built in 1881-2 for the stockbroker R.W. Elliston, Gledhill was designed by the Liverpool architect J. Francis Doyle. It is in the fashionable 'Old English' style that Doyle learned from Richard Norman Shaw. The chemical manufacturer Andrew Kurtz saw it under construction and described it unsympathetically in his diary: 'Went to look at the pretentious-looking house at the entrance of the park & to my astonishment hear it is being built by "young" Elliston who was a needy vagabond the other day & who has made a grand coup on the Stock Exchange! It seems a curiously arranged, straggling kind of mansion, with an infinity of odd corners & unsymmetrical rooms' *(Liverpool Libraries, Liverpool Record Office: 920 KUR 1/22, diary of A.G. Kurtz, 7 February 1882).*

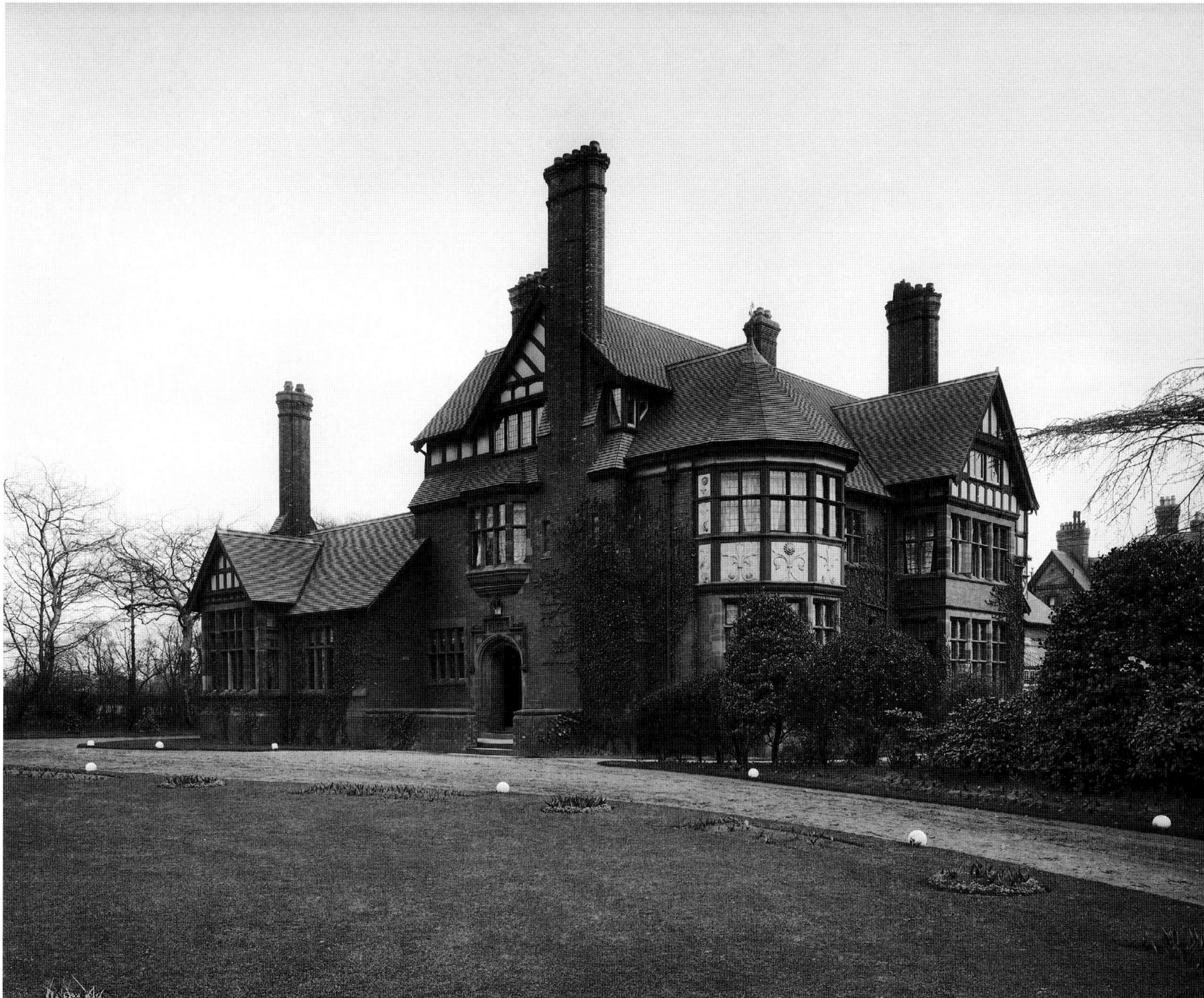

40. The entrance hall, Gledhill, April 1904 (BL 18184)

There are two distinct layers of decoration in this room. The arched inglenook and panelled chimneypiece were presumably part of J. Francis Doyle's original 1881-2 design for the house. Superimposed on them is a 'Burmese' mantelshelf, and the same oriental taste extends to the centre table and mirror. These features were probably added for J.A.F. Aspinall, general manager of the Lancashire and Yorkshire Railway, who moved into Gledhill in about 1900.

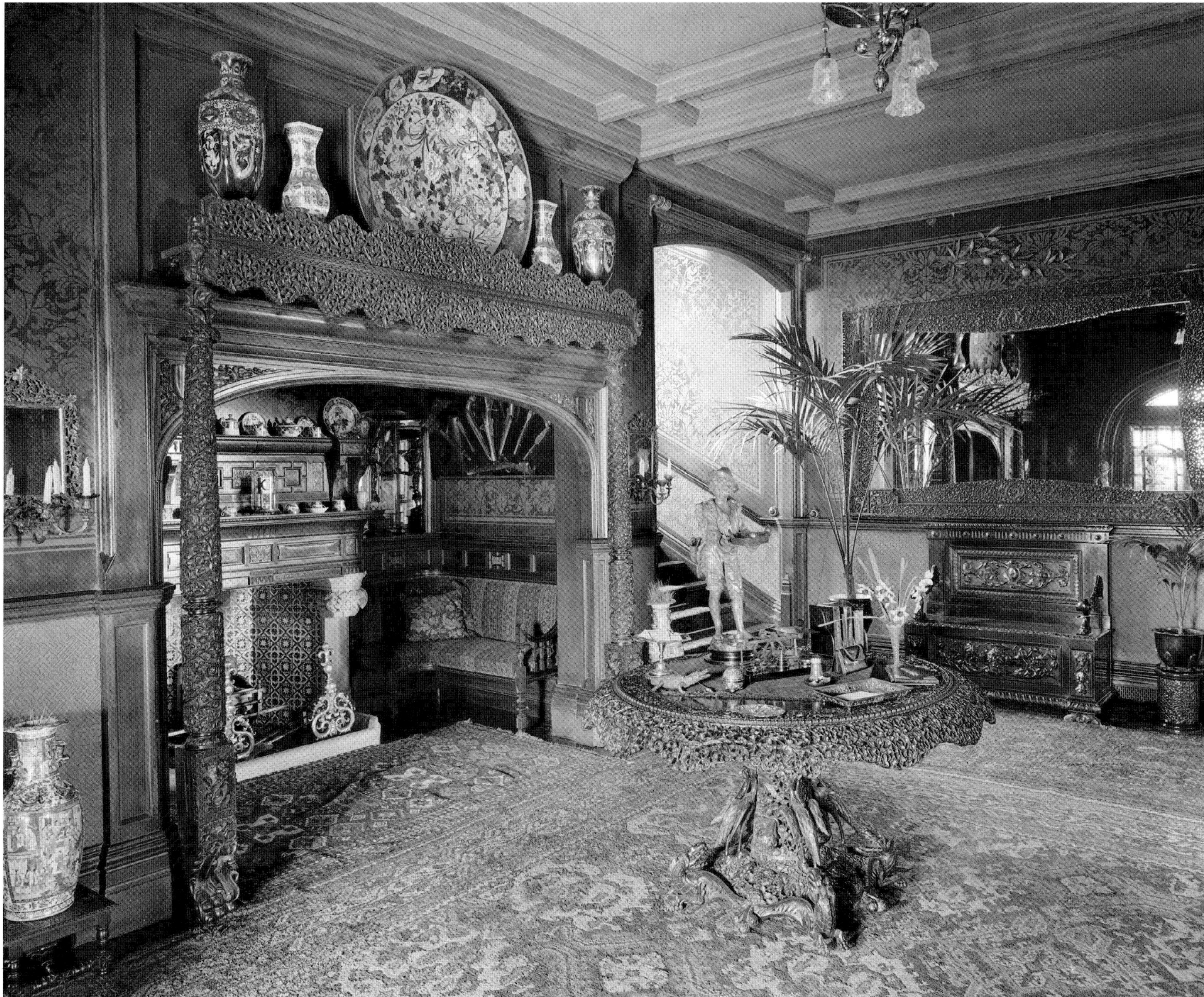

41. The entrance hall, Mere Hall, Noctorum, July 1904 (BL 18424)

The elevated ridge of Noctorum on the fringes of Birkenhead has splendid views across the Wirral to North Wales. It was developed in the 1880s and 90s with large houses for Liverpool businessmen, several of which were designed by the prolific Liverpool architect Edmund Kirby. Mere Hall is one of the earliest, built in about 1880 for the maritime solicitor John Gray Hill. Hill bought antique panelling for this room, which Kirby ingeniously fitted into its new setting: the cornice and the pairs of baroque pilasters are old, but the fire surround is Kirby's own. Hill and his artist wife were enthusiasts for the Middle East – they owned a house in Jerusalem – and this taste is reflected in the rug and other ornaments. It is also evident in the book prominently placed on the table – *The Life of the Master* by Ian Maclaren (the pen name of John Watson, minister of Sefton Park Presbyterian Church). Published in 1901, this study of Christ was illustrated with carefully researched pictures of the Holy Land by C.K. Linson.

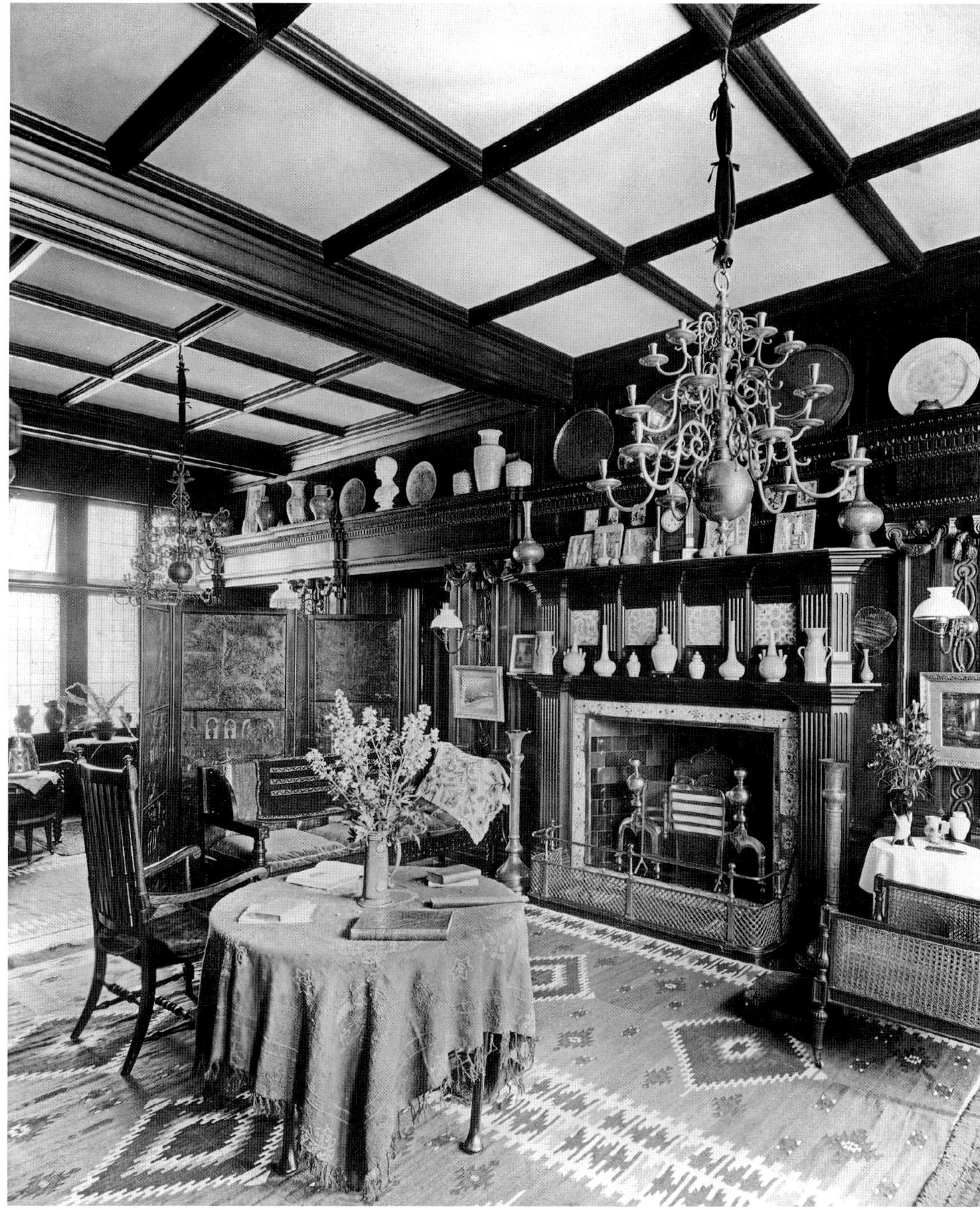

42. The dining room, Mere Hall, July 1904 (BL 18433)

Describing another of Edmund Kirby's Noctorum houses, Ulverscroft, a local magazine remarked that 'it shows itself to be the abode of a man of taste, who consults the unities, and who will, when he can, have all things about him in harmony with each other. [It] is newly and handsomely furnished in the modern style. The modern style may, perhaps, be best described as an artistic imitation of the old style, and a vast improvement upon it' (*Liberal Review*, 4 June 1881). The same description would apply equally to Mere Hall. Every detail of the dining room is carefully calculated for its visual effect. The pictures, the silver on the sideboard and the oriental porcelain over the door are all arranged in balanced groups, items of different styles and periods being blended into a unified whole.

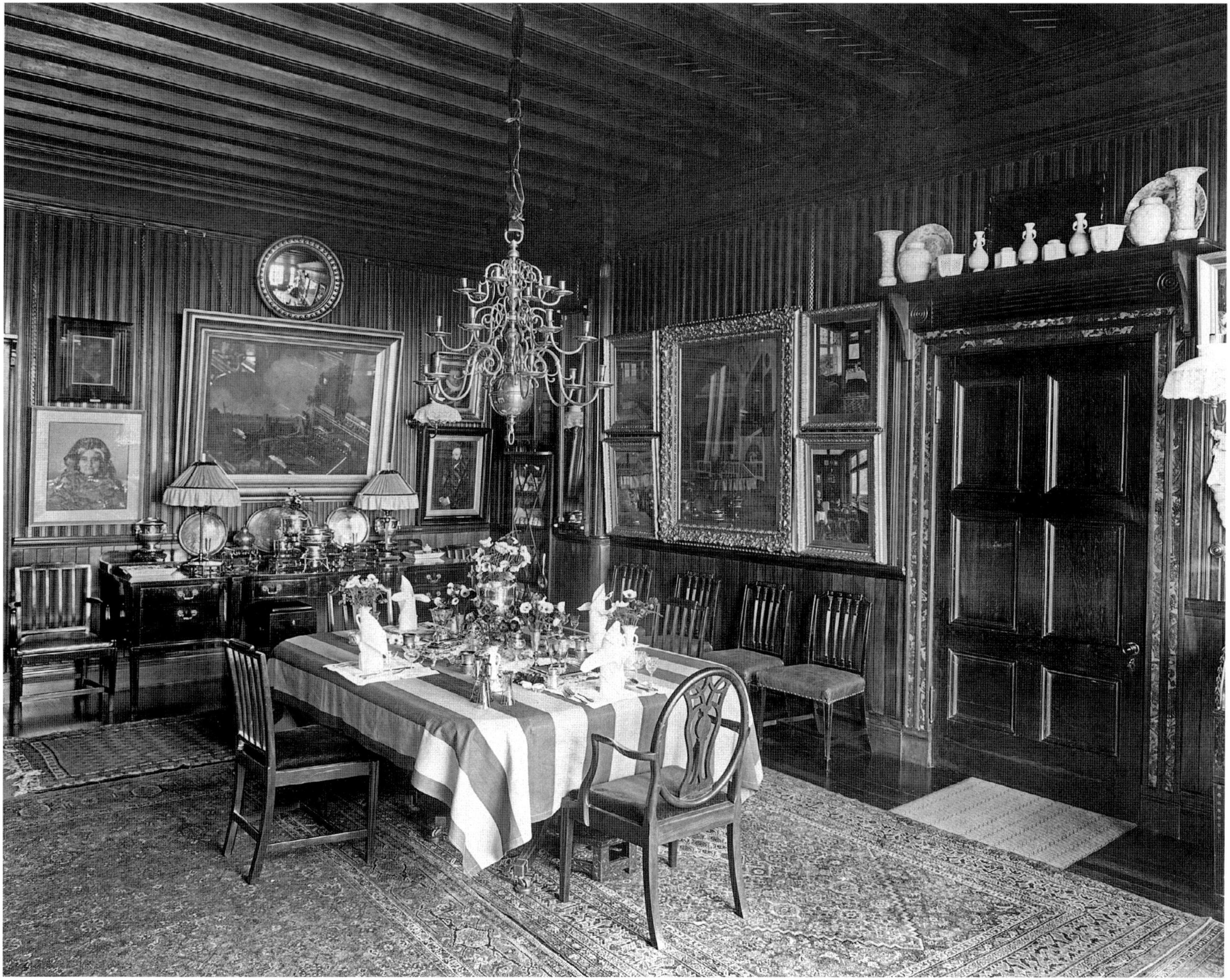

43. The landing, Wilton Grange, Meols Drive, West Kirby, 1914 (BL 22891)

Wilton Grange was built around 1905 by the brewer William E. Cain. His father, Robert Cain, founded the Mersey Brewery and built the famous Philharmonic Hotel in Liverpool's Hope Street. The Wirral became popular with commuters as rail links with Liverpool improved in the late nineteenth century, especially after electrification of the under-river Mersey Railway in 1903.

In John Owen's 1921 novel of commercial Liverpool, *The Cotton Broker*, one of the characters commutes to work from the Wirral, where he lives in a large house 'elaborate with oak beams and an improvised air of antiquity'. Wilton Grange seems to have been just such a house. The suit of armour, family portraits and seventeenth-century-style furniture suggest that this is the ancient seat of an aristocratic family, not the modern home of a prosperous brewer.

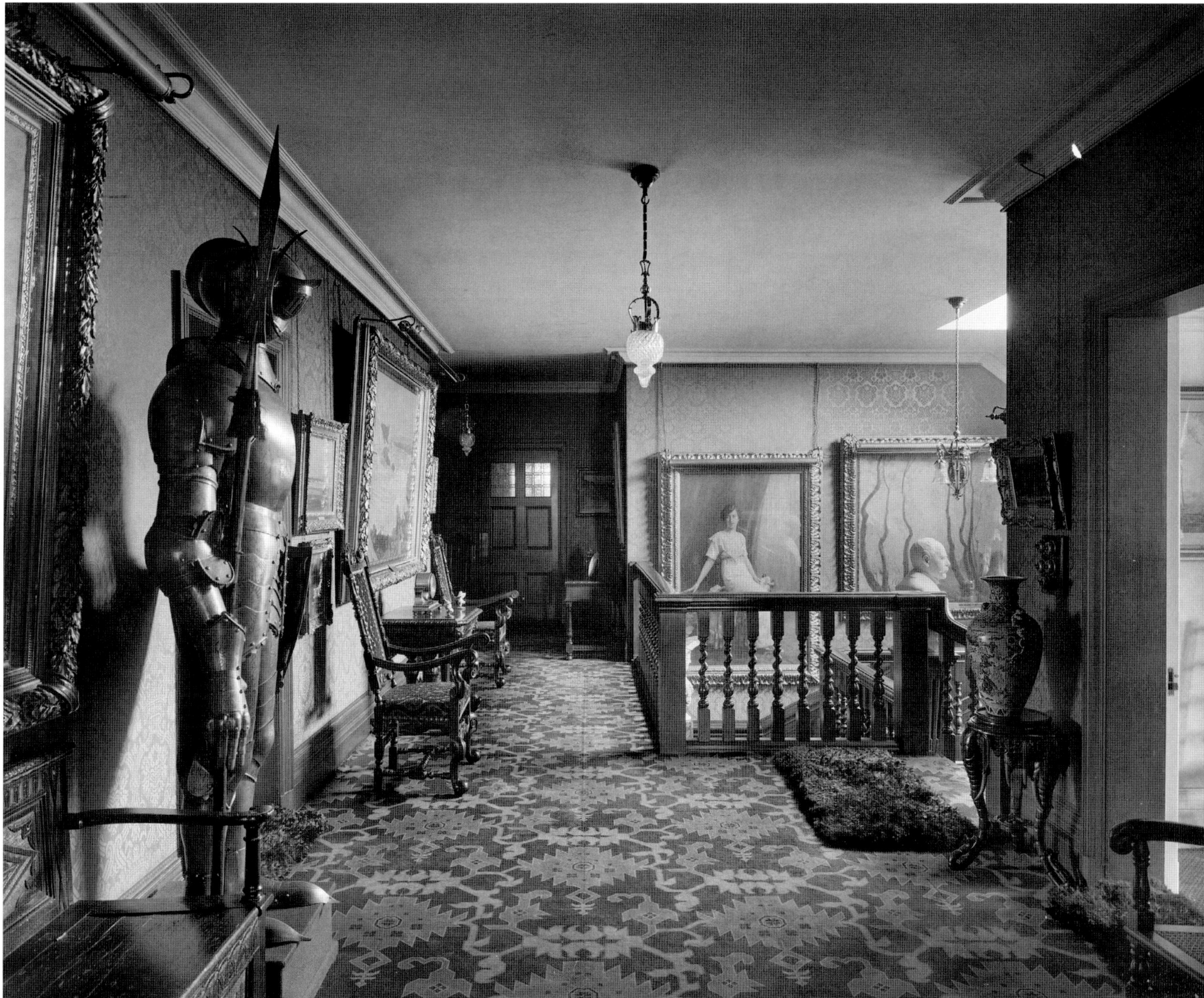

44. Miss Cain's bedroom, Wilton Grange, 1914 (BL 22893)

This room was occupied by William E. Cain's only daughter, Dorothy Mary, who would have been about twenty-one when the photograph was taken. In general, early-twentieth-century taste rejected the dark colours, rich patterns and heavy draperies of the nineteenth century. This bedroom is light and bright, but still very full of furniture and possessions, including not one but two dressing tables.

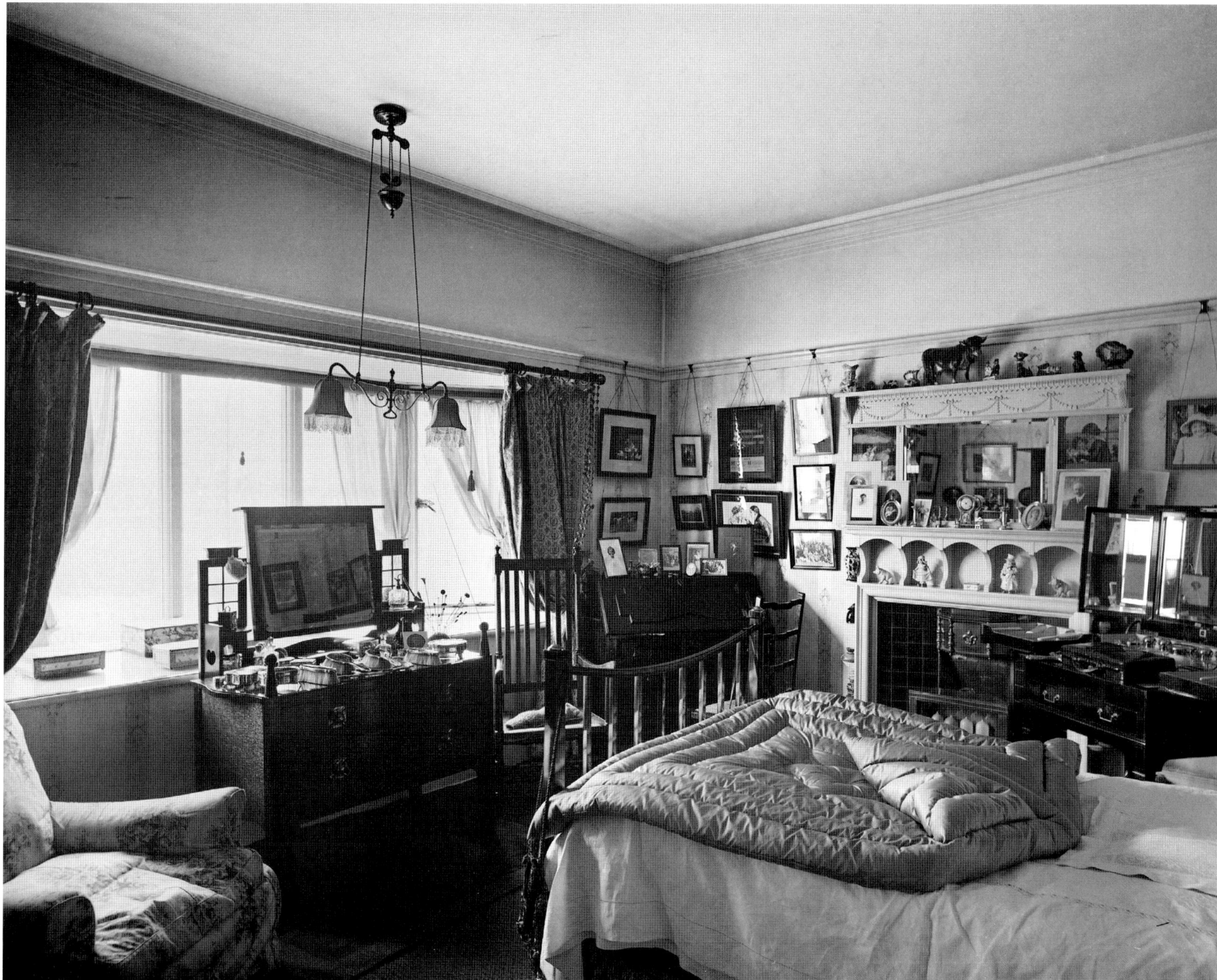

45. Uplands, Burbo Bank Road North, Blundellsands, 1916 (BL 23620/2)

Lying just north of Waterloo, with a convenient rail link to Liverpool, Blundellsands developed as an affluent commuter suburb from the 1860s onwards. Among the earliest houses was Uplands, in existence by 1870, when it was occupied by the timber merchant Joseph Gardner. Like many of its neighbours it was of red brick with bands of blue and white, a combination ridiculed as the 'streaky bacon style' by critics at the time. Sea views were a special attraction of Blundellsands – 'probably no place in the United Kingdom possesses a finer marine prospect' wrote Sir William B. Forwood, who lived there from 1871 to 1898 – and Uplands had a turret from which to enjoy them. The foreshore also provided space for recreation: 'on the beach', said the satirical magazine *Porcupine* in 1867, 'the aristocracy of Waterloo enliven the scene with equestrian performances.' But the location also had its dangers, and in the early twentieth century a number of the waterfront houses were undermined by the sea and had to be demolished. By the time this photograph was taken Uplands was occupied by Andrew D. Mearns, general manager of the Cunard Steamship Co.

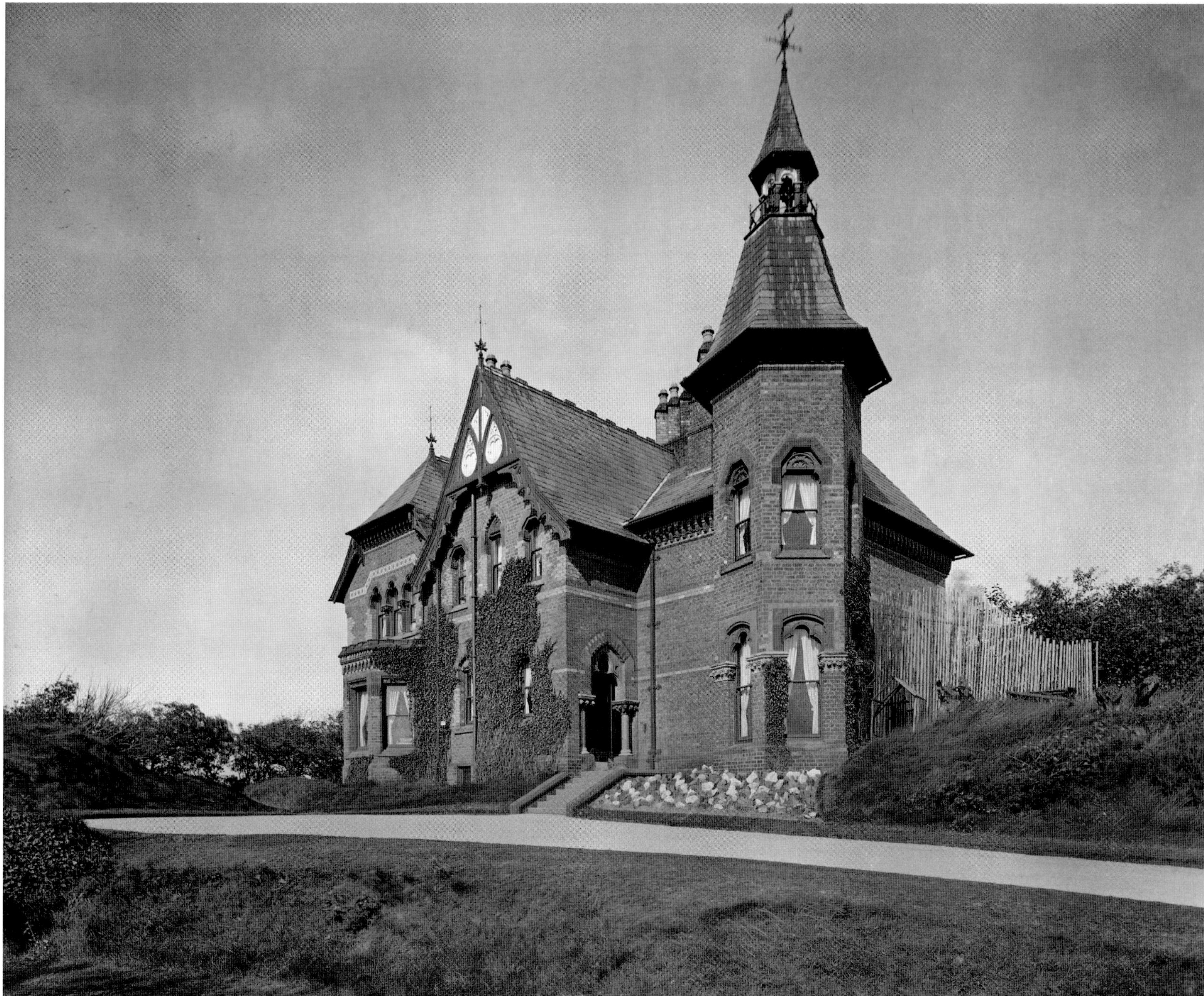

46. Park Lea, Fulwood Park, Aigburth, 1916 (BL 23621/3)

Fulwood Park was laid out in the 1840s as an exclusive residential street, secure behind its own lodge and gates. In *Liverpool's Legion of Honour* (an 1893 'Who's Who' of leading citizens) B.G. Orchard wrote that 'to live [...] even in its smallest house, has long been suggestive of ultra social importance'. Park Lea was not the smallest house in Fulwood Park, and its grounds were among the most extensive: the original owner, the lawyer Thomas Avison, appears to have leased a double plot, building his house on half and keeping the rest as gardens. The bow-fronted conservatory enjoyed views over this gently sloping landscape.

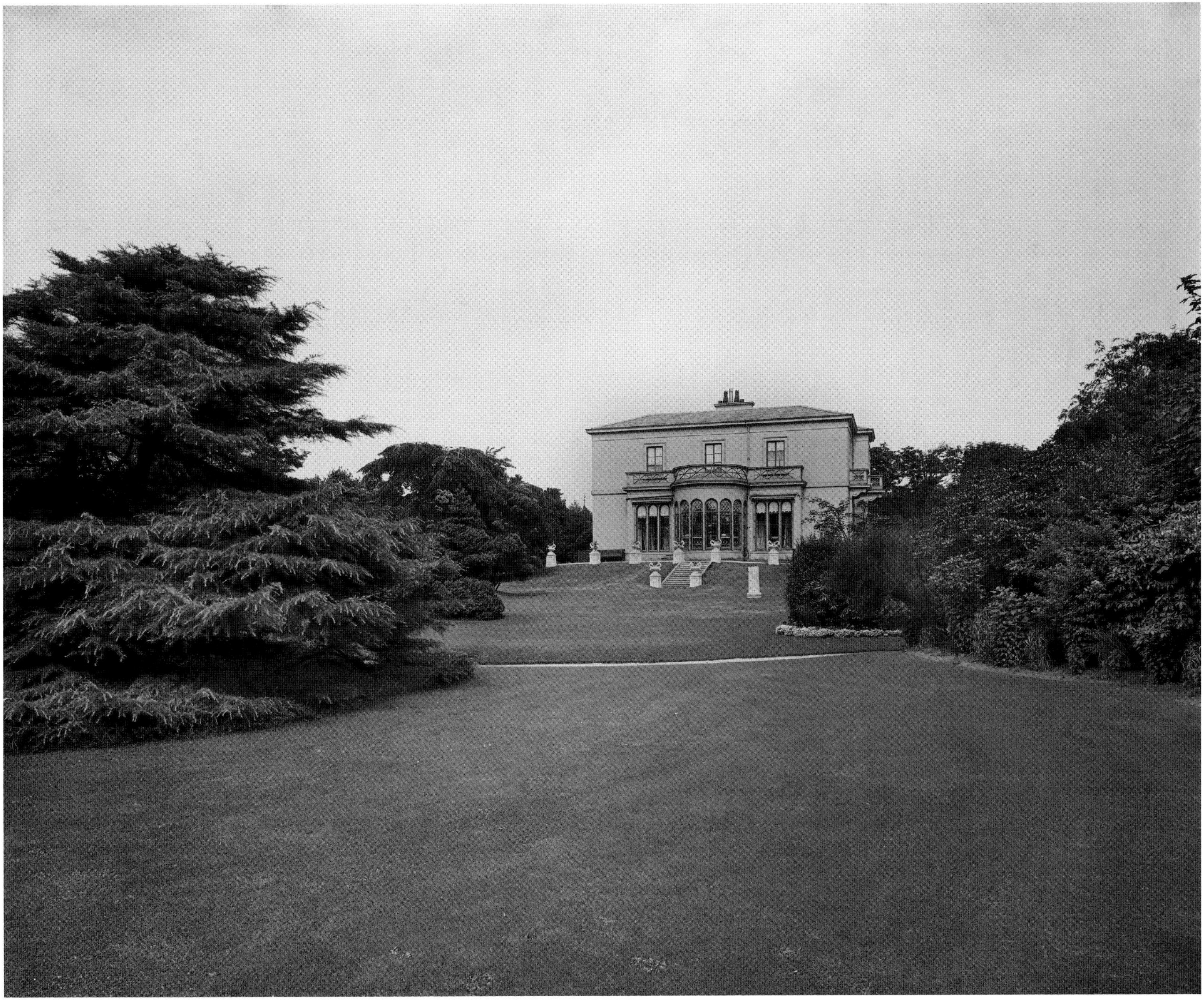

47. The entrance hall, Park Lea, 1916 (BL 23621/13)

In about 1910 Park Lea became the home of Richard J. Blackler, owner of Blackler's department store at the corner of Elliot Street and Great Charlotte Street in Liverpool city centre. When Bedford Lemere photographed the house it had been newly furnished by Waring & Gillow. The entrance hall is as densely packed as any Victorian interior with furniture, paintings and bronzes jostling for attention – almost like a department store, in fact.

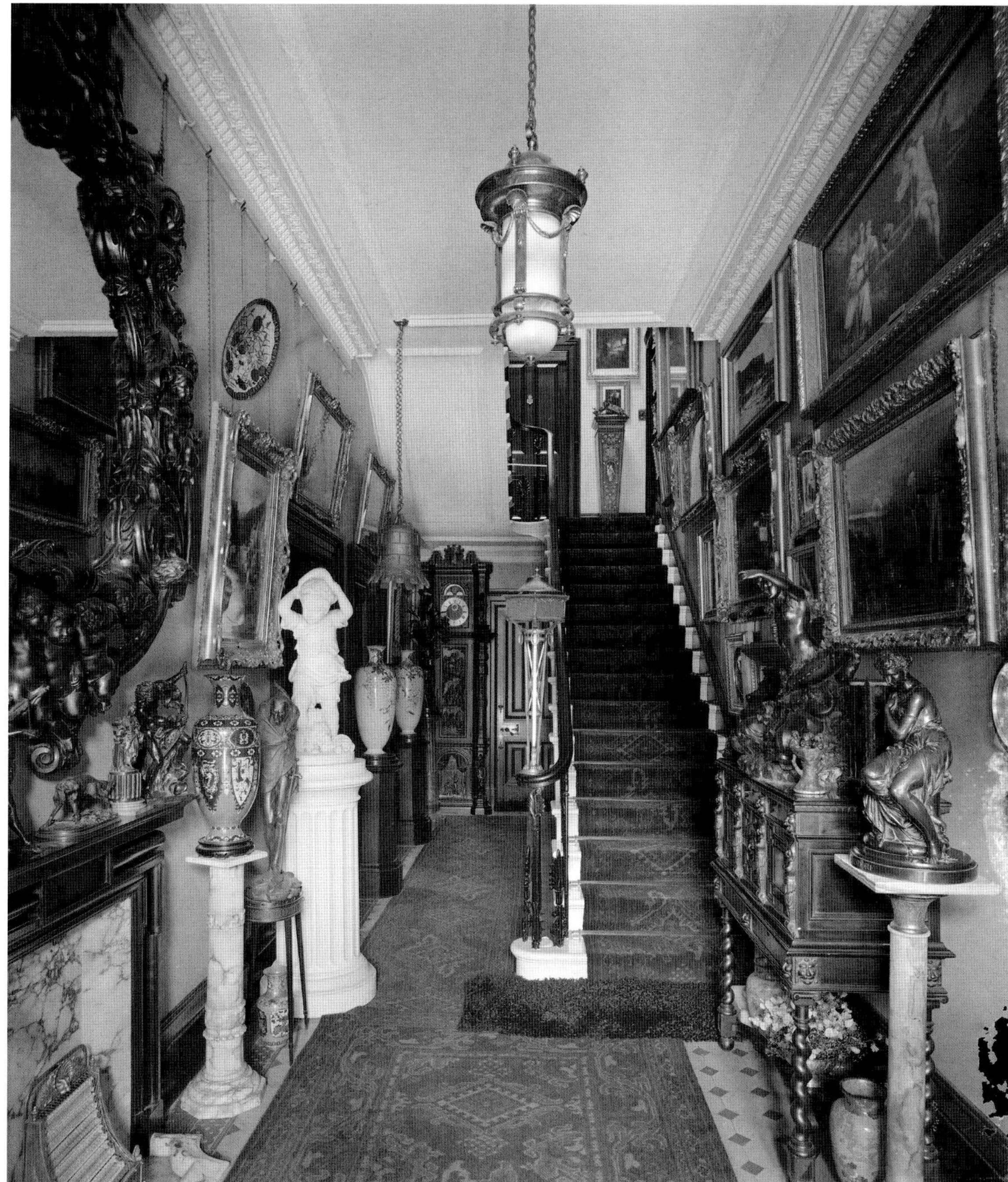

106

48. Mrs Blackler's bathroom, Park Lea, 1916 (BL 23621/23)

Mrs Blackler's marble-lined bathroom was equipped with weighing scales, an electric fire and a toilet discreetly hidden by a cane armchair.

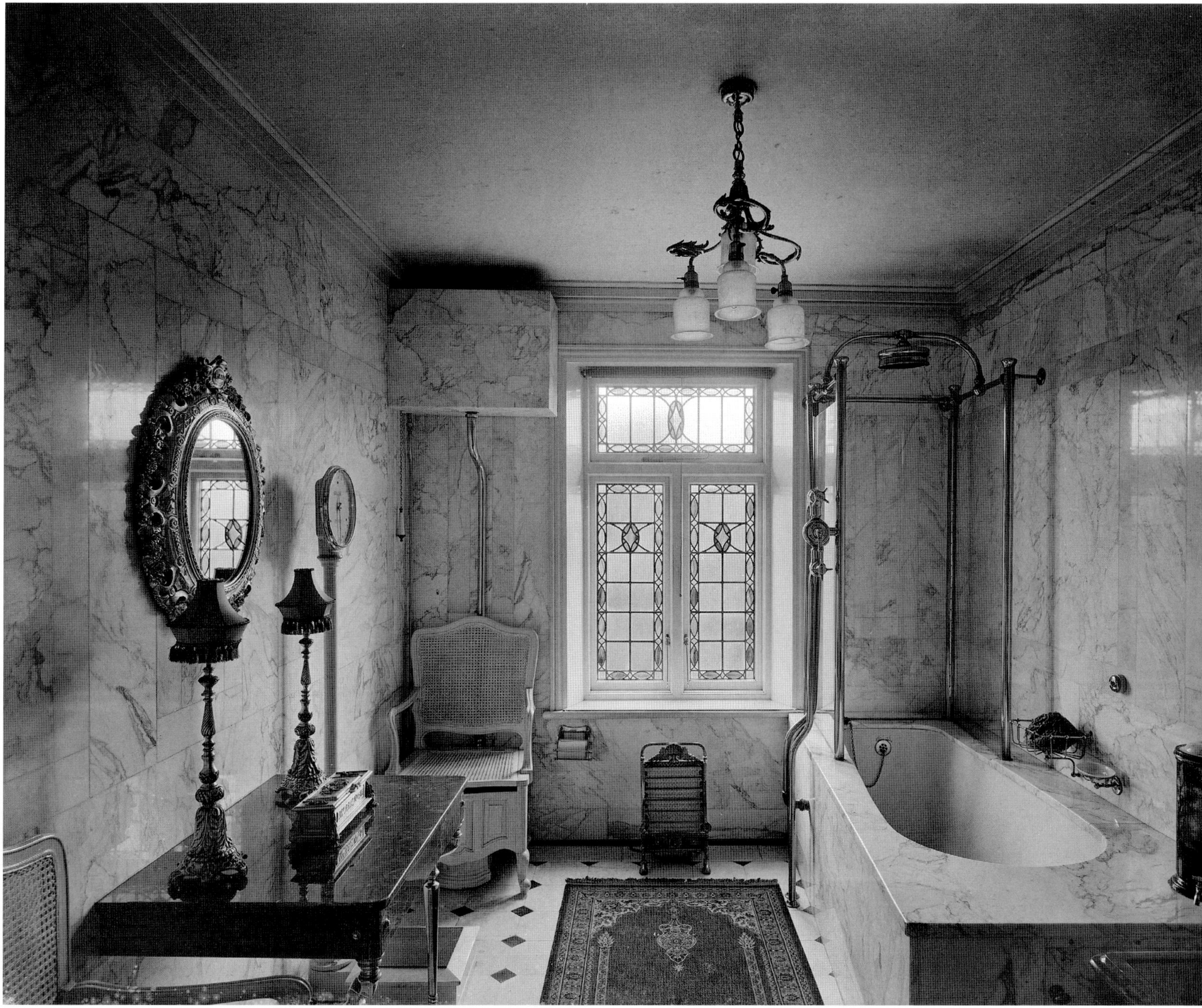

49. Orleans House, Aigburth Drive, 1916 (BL 23624/1)

One of the largest of the villas overlooking Sefton Park, Orleans House was built for the cotton merchant Benjamin Newgass around 1878. It was designed by Charles Z. Hermann, a Liverpool architect and property developer responsible for some of the earliest park-side housing. The villas were quite closely spaced, but at the front they enjoyed open views over the park. Orleans House also had a spacious garden at the back, with extensive glasshouses and a croquet lawn. The domed conservatory may be the 'rose house' for which a new occupier, the stockbroker Walter C. Clark, obtained planning permission in 1884. A simpler greenhouse is just visible on the left. Screened by shrubbery, it must have belonged to the kitchen garden.

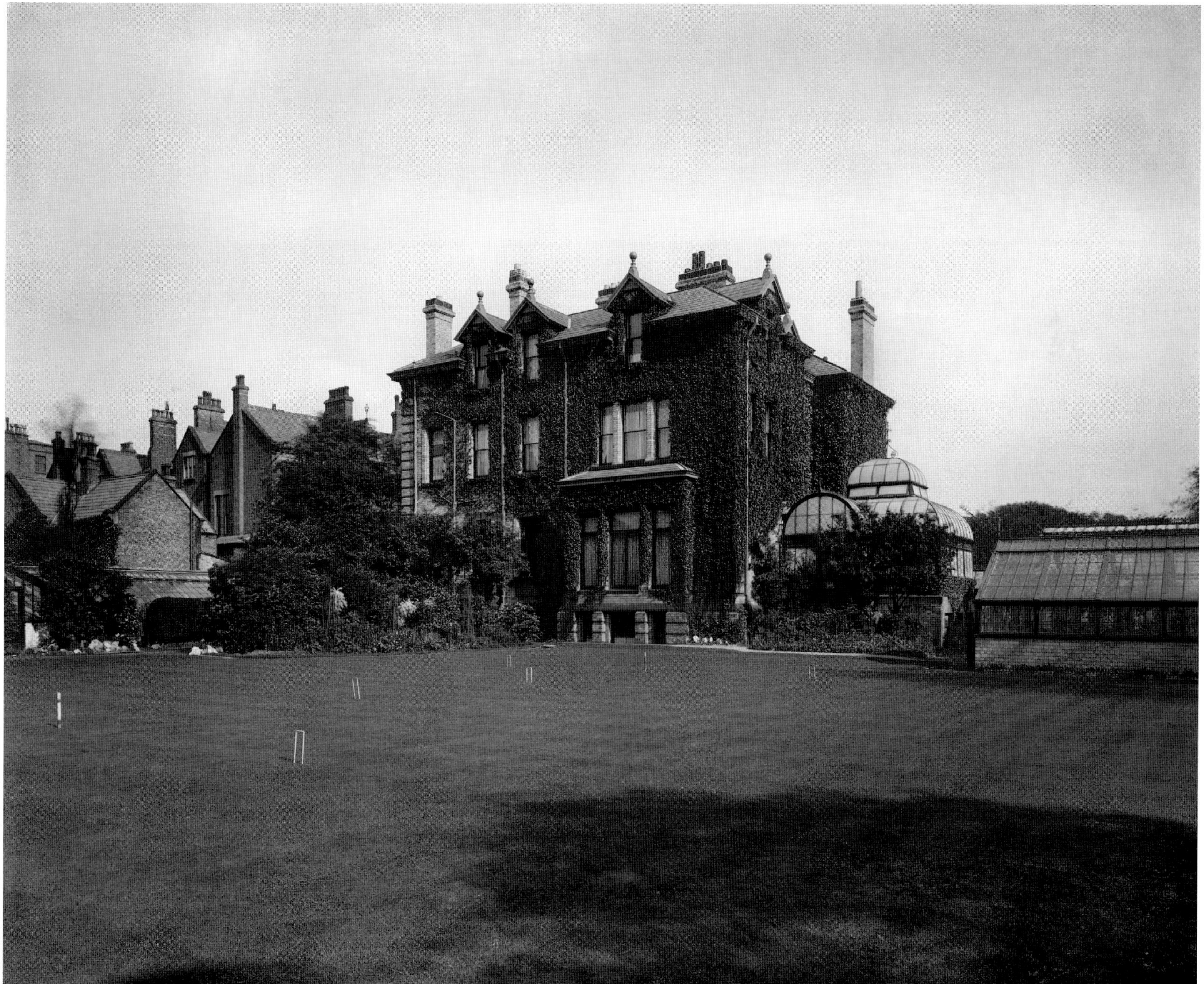

50. The entrance hall, Orleans House, 1916 (BL 23625)

Though many of the houses bordering Sefton Park survive, the interiors have generally been subdivided. This entrance hall shows the scale of their reception and circulation spaces – impressive when used for entertaining, but cavernous for ordinary domestic purposes. After visiting another of the park-side villas – The Towers in Ullet Road – Andrew Kurtz remarked in his diary: 'What an "Institution" [it] looks in the day time! The corridor – so splendid when lighted up & filled with company – looks a desert by daylight' *(Liverpool Libraries, Liverpool Record Office: 920 KUR 1/22, diary of A.G. Kurtz, 24 December 1882).*

By the time Bedford Lemere photographed it, Orleans House was occupied by Valdemar G. Graae, a Danish margarine manufacturer. The area had long been noted for its cosmopolitan population and as late as 1921 Charles Reilly called it 'the Sefton Park foreign quarter'.

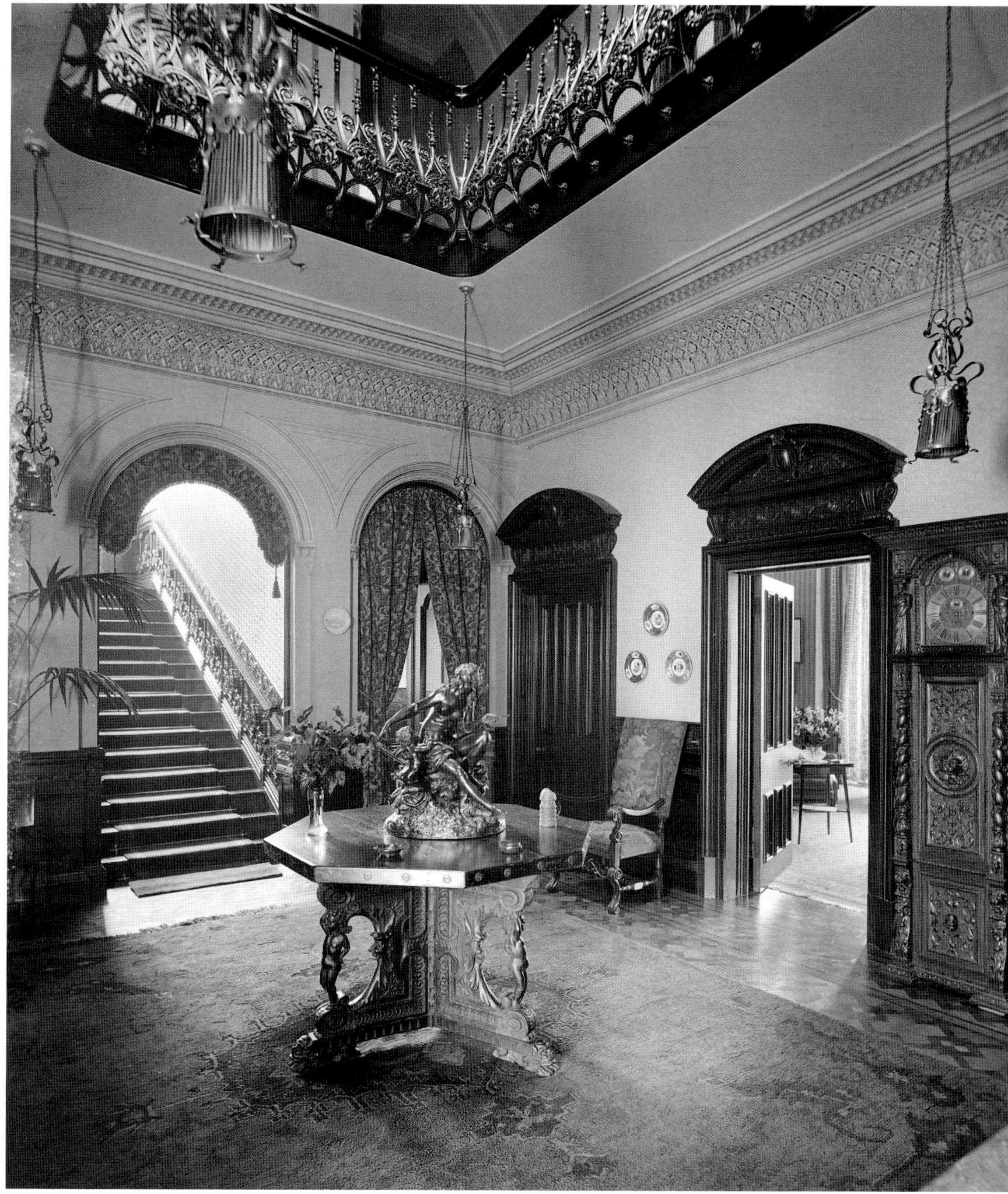

Acknowledgements

Photographs reproduced by permission of English Heritage.NMR

ENGLISH HERITAGE
NATIONAL MONUMENTS RECORD

The images in this publication are part of the Bedford Lemere Collection, a unique record of architecture and design in the nineteenth and early twentieth centuries. The Collection is held as part of the National Monuments Record, the public archive of English Heritage.

The NMR holds over 8 million photographs dating from the 1840s to the present day that record England's architecture and archaeology from the ground and from the air. For more information contact:

NMR Enquiry & Research Services
National Monuments Record Centre
Kemble Drive, Swindon SN2 2GZ

Tel: 01793 414600 Fax: 01793 414606
Email: nmrinfo@english-heritage.org.uk

To see over 45,000 of these images please go to
www.english-heritage.org.uk/viewfinder

This publication is an outcome of the University of Liverpool's Mercantile Liverpool Project, which is funded by the Leverhulme Trust, English Heritage, the Philip Holt Trust, and Liverpool City Council's World Heritage Site.

The author would like to thank Anne Woodward, Caroline Craggs, Ian Leith, Sandra Penketh, Steven Brookes, Scott Carlin, Hilary de Bie, Roger Hull, Simon Poe, Andrew Saint, Julian Treuherz and the staff of the Liverpool Record Office for their help.